外邦粹礼

桂林博物馆藏外宾礼品

Waibang Cuili
Guilin Bowuguan Cang Waibin Lipin

主　编　唐春松
副主编　韦卫能　孙明光　洪德善　唐奇岭

GUANGXI NORMAL UNIVERSITY PRESS
广西师范大学出版社　·桂林·

序　言

桂林是世界知名的风景旅游城市，桂林的奇山秀水和悠久的历史文明魅力赢得了世界的向往。自20世纪70年代以来，世界各国的国家元首及政府首脑百余人，以及国际友人数百万人曾到桂林参观访问。改革开放后，桂林的大门进一步向世界敞开，每年到访的四海宾朋络绎不绝。此外，我市的有关部门机构也曾多次组团访问世界各国。1979年至1997年间，桂林先后与日本的熊本市、新西兰的黑斯廷斯市、美国的奥兰多市和韩国的济州市结为友好城市，各友城之间往来交流日益密切。桂林人民与世界各国人民的友好交流与日俱增，相互赠送的礼品也逐渐多起来。为了更好地展示桂林人民与各国人民的友好交流，中共桂林市委、桂林市人民政府一致决定，由桂林市人民政府外事办公室将这些礼品移交给桂林博物馆作为收藏和展出之用。三十多年来，桂林博物馆珍藏了世界各国人民赠送我市的国际友谊礼品近三千件（套）。这些礼品极具世界各国的文化特色，是各国风情的一个缩影，体现出五大洲的民俗风情，印证和记录着桂林与世界人民友好交往的步履，堪称桂林历史文化名城的又一面镜子。

这些琳琅满目的礼品造型别致、制作精美，大多带有明显的国家特征，且一件件藏品的背后还有着一个个鲜为人知的故事。这些藏品，不仅有小如鸡蛋的墨西哥牛仔工艺小草帽，也有重达300多千克的韩国济州岛石头翁；有短仅盈寸的米粒微雕，也有长逾4米的日本鲤鱼旗；有古朴的喀麦隆仿古铜雕，也有比利时所赠精致传神的绘画作品等，令人目不暇接。

1983年，巴基斯坦齐亚哈克总统赠送的玉盒、玉台灯庄重典雅，见证了中巴两国人民源远流长的深厚友谊。

1977年5月，与周总理交情很深的缅甸总统吴奈温将军来桂林，赠送了鎏金漆器和贝壳茶盒，既反映出中缅两国人民长期团结战斗的友谊，也展示了缅甸悠久的佛教文化传统。

与我国一衣带水的日本，其文化与中国有着千丝万缕的联系，也有难于化解的恩怨。1984年4月，日本画展团赠送的一幅山水画，画面上岚山的樱花遍山盈野，白雾萦绕，从峰壑间流出的桂川河水由渡月桥穿过，桥边立着一块碑，碑上刻着“日中不再战”。作者直外生田在画中题诗一首：“岚峡风光一段奇，龟山公苑立诗碑。桂川桥畔老僧碣，万世日中交款基。”这幅画是日本京都府京都市岚山脚下的实景写生，桂川中流的中之岛上，矗立着一块巨石，赫然镌刻着“日中不再战”五个大字，后面的碑文记载了1968年在纪念日中战争30周年时，由日中不再战运动京都执行委员会立。这里的气氛显然与靖国神社形成强烈的对比，但愿两国如碑所刻，永不再战。

泰国的纸雕“象战”镜屏，仿佛诉说着泰国人民为抵御侵略者而进行的斗争。泰国历史上最著名的一次象战发生在1592年1月25日，是泰王纳黎萱同缅甸王子的一次战斗。当时，缅甸王子统率两路大军分别向泰国京都挺进，双方在素攀府境内展开决战。泰王抓住时机将缅甸王子砍死在象颈之上。缅军见主帅已死，无心再战，败阵而回。从此，纳黎萱王名声大振。在以后的150年内，缅甸没有再进犯泰国。此次象战史称“象阵战”。为纪念这次象战，素攀府建了象战塔，1月25日这一天后来被定为泰国的军队节。

1974年，越南民主共和国所赠的一批磨漆画独具特色，闻名于世。最值得一提的是，漆艺由中国传到越南，在20世纪初发展出了磨漆画，并于该世纪下半叶回传中国。以前，漆画在中国是附属于漆器的，例如在屏风或首饰盒上绘制人物花鸟图案，没有独立的艺术地位。但是越南艺术家的努力使磨漆画脱离了工艺美术品，成为一个独立的画种，甚至成为越南的国画，在世界赢得广泛声誉。

越南礼品中还有两件用美国弹片制作的人物雕像，反映了越南抗美时代的鲜明特色。在厚约一厘米、巴掌大的两块弹片上，雕刻着越军战士在热带丛林中英勇作战的情景。这也使人回想起20世纪六七十年代，桂林人民为支援越南人民的抗美战争所做出的贡献和付出。

1977年，喀麦隆总统阿希乔赠送给桂林一套充满非洲原始部落社会风俗、宗教信仰、传奇色彩与美学观念的铜面具、铜钟铃、铜骑士、蛇皮纹串珠铁手杖仿制品。其中的每一个雕刻图案都有其特定的寓意，蕴含着深层的文化记忆。

1976年，美国前总统尼克松所送的两件礼物——一件绘有美丽天鹅的瓷盘和一件憨态可掬的瓷熊猫，则见证了中美建交历史，寓意深远。据说，当时尼克松访华到桂林之前曾提出了种种礼物的设想。为了对桂林人民表示敬意，美方最后选定了瓷熊猫作为礼物。熊猫习性温和、憨态可掬、举止大方，即使在异国他乡也毫不拘束，自由自在，深受美利坚民族的喜爱。尼克松将“熊猫”不远万里从美国送回它的家乡，象征着和平、善良和友谊。

1985年5月15日，在桂林与美国奥兰多结为友好城市的签字仪式上，奥兰多市长所赠的镀金奥兰多市城门钥匙，堪称是赠送给桂林人民最珍贵的礼品。据说，历史上西方每座城市都有自己的城门钥匙。城市钥匙是一种象征式的物件，代表该城市的最高荣誉。在外国很多大城市，市长会向对国家社会有功之人士颁赠城市钥匙，以示褒扬，此人也成为荣誉市民。在国际上，有一种来源于古代欧洲的赠送金钥匙礼节。当外国贵宾访问某一城市时，该城的最高执政长官将城门的金钥匙赠送给外国贵宾，以此表示尊敬和欢迎，以及作为高度信任和亲密无间的友谊象征。奥兰多市长把镀金的城门钥匙交给桂林人民，无私地表示了其与桂林人民的亲近，并祝愿桂林人民打开智慧的城门，通往更美好和光明的世界。

中国与世界各国的友好往来和文化交流源远流长，桂林博物馆是全国最早收藏展示国际友谊礼品的博物馆。桂林博物馆所藏礼品数量和种类之丰富在全国各大中城市中名列前茅，目前藏品量仅次于北京国际友谊博物馆和中国人民革命军事博物馆，成为桂林博物馆中很能表现桂林特色的专项藏品。这些精妙绝伦的礼品，是桂林人民与世界各国人民友好往来的见证，充分显示出桂林在国际交往中的重要地位，在中外友好交流史上留下了举足轻重的一页。感谢中共桂林市委、桂林市人民政府的英明决策，也感谢桂林市人民政府外事办公室的长期支持，才有了如今桂林博物馆琳琅满目的精美外宾礼品。还要感谢广西师范大学出版社的辛勤努力，使这本精美图录顺利与读者见面。让我们保护好这些珍贵的藏品，向世人充分展示桂林历史文化名城的无穷魅力。

桂林博物馆馆长 唐春松

2014年10月

Preface

As a world-famous city known for its scenery and tourism, Guilin has gained the world favor with its extraordinary landscape and long history. Since the 1970s, over 100 national leaders and government heads from different countries as well as millions of international friends had visited Guilin. After China's reform and opening up, the gate of Guilin opens wider to the outside world, and numerous guests and friends from every corner of the world stream into Guilin each year. In return, the relative organizations and departments of Guilin organize delegations to visit foreign countries. During the period from 1979 to 1997, Guilin established a friendly relationship as Sister Cities with Kumamoto City of Japan, Hastings City of New Zealand, Orlando City of America and Jeju City of Korea successively, and the exchange and communication between the cities became increasingly closer. Along with the growing of the friendly contact between Guilin people and people across the world, the gifts presented by each other gradually increase. To better demonstrate the friendly ties between Guilin people and people from other countries, Guilin Municipal Party Committee and Guilin Municipal People's Government made the unanimous decision that the gifts would be turned over by Foreign Affairs Office of the People's Government of Guilin Municipality to Guilin Museum for collection and exhibition. During the over 30 years, Guilin Museum has collected nearly 3,000 international friendly gifts presented by people from other countries. With distinctive exotic cultural characteristics, these gifts are an epitome of the styles of different countries. They not merely present the folk customs and styles of the five continents, but also corroborate and record the footsteps of the friendly ties between Guilin people and people across the world. Therefore, it is no exaggeration to say the foreign gifts are another mirror of Guilin, the noted historical and cultural city.

Boasting elegant style and exquisite making, these beautiful gifts mostly have distinct national features and have rarely known stories behind them. Of the collections, there's not merely Mexican jean straw hat as small as an egg, but also stone sculpture of Dolharubang which weighs up to over 300 kilograms; there's not merely inch-long grain micro-carving, but Japanese salmon flag with the length of over 4 meters as well; there's classic Cameroon bronze sculpture in the style of the ancients as well as the vivid, exquisite paintings presented by Belgium. The various, exquisite gifts impress and dazzle people greatly.

Decent and elegant, the jade case and jade lamp presented by Pakistan President Zia-ul-Haq in 1983 witness the long, profound friendship between Chinese people and Pakistan people.

Having a sound relationship with Premier Zhou Enlai, General Ne Win, Prime Minister of Burma came to Guilin in May, 1977, and presented gilded lacquer ware and shell tea box, not merely reflecting the friendship between Chinese people and Burmese people which was forged during the long term solidarity and struggle, but also presenting Burma's long-standing Buddhism cultural tradition.

Separated from China with a narrow strip of water, Japan has countless ties with China in culture.

Meanwhile, there's also resentment between China and Japan which could hardly be resolved. In April, 1984, Japanese Painting Exhibition Delegation presented a landscape painting to Guilin. On the painting, Arashiyama cherries blossom all over the mountains and plains, white fog hovers, Katsura River waters flow from the peaks and ravines and cross Togetsu Bridge, besides which stands a stone tablet, on which is carved "no war between Japan and China". There's also a poem inscribed by the painter: "Amid the extraordinary Arashiyama scenery, stands the inscribed stone tablet in Kameyama Park. On the Old Monk Stone Tablet besides the bridge along Katsura River, starts the forever friendship between Japan and China." This painting depicts the scenery at the foot of Arashiyama in Kyoto City of Kyoto Prefecture of Japan. In Nakanoshima at the midstream of Katsura River stands a giant rock, on which 5 characters are inscribed impressively: "no war between Japan and China". The inscription reads: Inscribed in 1968, the 30th anniversary of Japan-China War, erected by "No War between Japan and China" Campaign Kyoto Executive Committee. The atmosphere forms a striking contrast with Yasukuni Shrine. It is expected that the two countries would never fight with each other, just as the tablet inscription says.

Thailand paper engraving "elephant war" screen seems to recount the war Thai people waged against the invaders. The most renowned elephant war in Thailand history was the fight between Thailand King Naresuan and Burmese Prince on Jan 25, 1592. At that time, Burmese Prince led two troops to advance toward the capital of Thailand, and launched their decisive battle in Suphan Buri. Thailand King seized the opportunity and hacked Burmese Prince to death at the elephant neck. Seeing the general did, the Burmese army had no intention to fight; they lost the battle and fled away. Since then, Naresuan gained considerable fame. During the 150 years afterwards, Burma didn't invade Thailand. For this reason, this war was called "elephant war" in history. To commemorate the war, Elephant War Tower was set up in Suphan Buri and Oct. 25 was designated as Thailand Army Day.

With distinctive features, the batch of lacquer pictures presented by the Socialist Republic of Vietnam in 1974 is well-known throughout the world. What's most worth mentioning, lacquer picture was developed in the beginning of the 20th century after lacquer artwork spread from China to Vietnam and spread back to China in the latter half of the 20th century. In the past, Chinese lacquer picture, like the figure and flower-bird pattern painted on the screen or jewelry box, is attached to lacquer ware and has no independent artistic identity. Nevertheless, under the endeavor of Vietnamese artists, lacquer picture detaches itself from handicrafts and becomes an independent picture type, even becomes the national painting of Vietnam, gaining widespread reputation in the world.

Of the Vietnamese gifts, there are two figure sculptures made from American bullets, which reflect the distinctive features of the period of Vietnamese War of Resistance against America. On the two 1-centimeter-thick, palm-big shell fragments is the carving of the situation when Vietnamese soldiers fought bravely in jungles. This recalls the contribution and dedication Guilin people had made during the Aiding Vietnam and Resisting America War during the 1960s and 1970s.

The set of bronze mask, bronze bell, bronze knight, imitation of iron cane with snake skin vein decorated with a string of beads presented by Cameroon President Ahidjo to Guilin in 1997 fully reflect the social custom, religious belief, legendary and aesthetic concept of African primitive tribes. Every carving pattern of the artworks has special implications and entails profound cultural memories.

The two gifts presented by former American President Nixon in 1976 — porcelain plate painted with swans and porcelain panda with an air of charming naivety — witness the history of the establishment of the diplomatic ties between China and America and have profound implications. It was said Nixon had proposed different assumptions of gifts before coming to China. Finally, to extend their sincere respect to Guilin, American sides chose porcelain panda. Mild, romantic, naive, panda leads an easy, free life even in foreign lands and is therefore quite popular among American people.

Nixon's long-distance journey to bring "panda" from America to its hometown is definitely a symbol of peace, kindness and friendship.

In the signing ceremony on which Guilin and Orlando established a friendship relation as Sister Cities on May 15, 1985, Orlando Mayor presented to Guilin a gilded Orlando City gate key, which could be regarded as the most valuable gift presented to Guilin people. It is said that every city in the west has its own city gate key. As a symbolic object, city key represents the highest honor of the city. In many big cities of foreign countries, to show his commendation, the mayor would present the city key to the person who makes great contribution to the country or society, and the one who receives the city key would become honorary citizen. The etiquette of presenting golden key originated from ancient Europe. When the distinguished foreign guests visit a city, the highest administrator of the city would present the golden key of city gate to the guests, in order to show his respect and welcome. In this sense, Orlando Mayor's presenting the gilt city gate key to Guilin people is a sincere expression of his closeness to Guilin people and his heartfelt wish that Guilin people would open the city gate of wisdom toward a better and more brilliant world.

The friendly contact and cultural communication between China and other foreign countries boast a long history. Guilin Museum is China's first museum which collects and exhibits international friendship gifts. In terms of the number and variety of the collected gifts, Guilin Museum stands at the head of the large and medium-sized cities. Presently, the number of the collected gifts is secondary only to that of International Friendship Museum and the Military Museum of the Chinese People's Revolution. As the specialized collections which well demonstrate Guilin's distinctive features, these wonderful gifts witness the friendly contact between Guilin people and people from other foreign countries and fully demonstrate the important position Guilin takes in international communication. They play an important role in Chinese-foreign friendship communication history. Heartfelt thanks should be extended to Guilin Municipal Party Committee and Guilin Municipal People's Government for their wise decision. Gratitude should also be given to Foreign Affairs Office of the People's Government of Guilin Municipality for their long-term support. It is just under their endeavor that Guilin Museum owns fascinating exquisite foreign guest gifts. Gratitude should also be extended to Guangxi Normal University Press. It is just under its diligent effort that this exquisite album could smoothly meet the readers. Let us preserve the precious collections and show the world the infinite charm of Guilin.

Guilin Museum Curator Tang Chunsong

October, 2014

目　录
Contents

外邦粹礼

——桂林博物馆藏外宾礼品

中国是具有五千年历史的文明古国，在世界上享有“中华礼仪之邦”的赞誉。“有朋自远方来，不亦乐乎”，“海内存知己，天涯若比邻”，“我们的朋友遍天下”，等等，这些耳熟能详的名言俗语，表达了中华民族对朋友的真挚情谊。心存敬意、与人为善、以和为贵，不仅是中华民族的价值观和行事方式，也是我们中华民族几千年文明传承延续下来的“为国以礼、人以仁贵”人文精神的体现。

1949年10月，新中国屹立于世界东方，结束了旧中国的百年屈辱外交，建立和发展了我国同世界各国的友好合作关系，历尽艰辛驰骋于国际舞台，广交天下朋友，开创了中国外交的新纪元。六十多年来，中国政府坚定不移地奉行独立自主的和平外交政策，维护世界和平与稳定，赢得了国际社会的广泛尊敬和信任。

为了配合国家整体外交，1973年，素有“山水甲天下”之美誉的国际旅游文化名城——桂林，向世界敞开了它的城门。来访外宾与日俱增，外事活动日渐增多。桂林以其独特的自然山水和历史文化赢得了世界的赞誉，再加上它在广西政治、文化发展中的特殊地位，因而成为广西最早建立外事机构的城市之一，成为中国政府接待外国友人的一个首选地。世界许多国家的元首和政府首脑在国事访问期间，专程前来桂林参观游览，仅美国就有五位总统在任职期间或任职前后访问过桂林。

四十多年来，桂林政府积极拓展对外交流合作渠道。1979年10月，在廖承志副委员长的亲切关怀下，桂林市首次与日本熊本市结成了国际友好城市，此后又陆续与新西兰、美国等多个国家的城市建立了国际友好城市。桂林与友好城市之间在经济、文化、教育、旅游、环保、科学技术、城市建设等多方面进行交流与合作，既增进了桂林与世界各国人民的相互了解和友谊，开拓了城市之间的合作领域，又扩大了桂林山水文化的国际影响力，促进了社会经济发展和文明进步。

据统计，自新中国成立以来，桂林接待了来自世界五大洲的150多位包括国家元首、政府首脑在内的各国政要，以及各界友好代表团和人士。美丽的桂林成为连接中国与世界的友谊桥梁，在新中国对外交流的舞台上谱写了一曲友谊和平的乐章。

随着区域交通、民族交往、文化艺术交流以及各阶层人士交际等的促进和发展，相互馈赠礼品成了上至外交礼仪、下至民间礼俗的一项重要内容。在对外交往中，访桂的世界各国政要、友好团体和人士以及友好城市，馈赠给桂林市政府及领导人大量的珍贵礼品。从20世纪70年代至今，凡外宾所赠送的礼品都登记造册入库交公，再由桂林市外事办公室移交桂林博物馆收藏。桂林博物馆至今已有外宾礼品近三千件（套），藏品数量仅次于国际友谊博物馆和中国人民革命军事博物馆，位居全国前三位，成为桂林博物馆独具地域特色的馆藏资源之一。这是桂林与世界各国人民友谊的结晶，是桂林与世界合作交流的实物见证，是桂林市对外工作所取得重大成果的有利展示，是欣赏异域文化精华、领略外国艺术风采的窗口。

桂林博物馆所藏的外宾礼品绚丽多彩、风格迥异、特色鲜明，包括金银器、铜铁器、玉石器、陶瓷器、玻璃器、漆器、牙骨器、木器、纺织品以及书画摄影等多个门类，颇具地域特色。它们代表了各国优秀的传统文化和独特的艺术风格，具有较高的历史价值、艺术价值和纪念象征意义，形象地反映了世界各民族的生产、生活、文化、艺术、宗教、服饰以及民间习俗等。每一件礼品都饱含着人类自然淳朴的创作情感，凝聚着世界人民的勤劳和智慧。古希腊诗人品达尔（Pindar）说过：“每一件礼物，无论大小，只要它蕴含感情，就是最好的礼物。”

在此，仅以筛选的近200件外宾礼品奉献给广大读者，希望观众通过观赏礼品、了解礼品，领略异域文化的风采，揭示人类文明所共同追求的永恒主题——和平与进步。愿这些来自远方的艺术瑰宝给广大观众带来温馨的友谊之情和难以忘怀的艺术享受。

Essence of Foreign Gifts

— Guilin Museum Collection of Foreign Gifts

As an ancient civilized country with a history of over 5,000 years, China enjoys the reputation of "land of etiquette". Well-known sayings such as "It is such a delight to have friends coming from afar","Long distance separates no bosom friends" and "We have friends all over the world" express Chinese people's heart-felt sincerity towards friends. Showing respect to others, being kind to others, taking harmony as the most precious are not merely Chinese people's value system and way of life, but also the representation of the human spirit of "governing the country by propriety, being a man by benevolence" which has been inherited through thousands of years of Chinese civilization.

In October, 1949, new China stood in the east of the world. It ended the century-old diplomacy humiliation, established and developed friendly cooperation with other countries throughout the world. Undergoing all kinds of hardship, new China galloped in the world stage and made friends widely, initiating a new era for Chinese diplomacy. For over 60 years, Chinese government has been unflinchingly adopting an independent foreign policy of peace to safeguard world peace and stability, and has won wide respect and trust from the international world.

As a renowned international tourism and culture city, Guilin enjoys the reputation of "Guilin landscape belittles those elsewhere". To meet the national diplomacy, Guilin opened its gate to the world in 1973. Since then, the visiting guests and foreign affairs have been increasing with each passing day. With its unique natural landscape and historical culture, Guilin gains the world acclaim. Besides, Guilin has special position in Guangxi political and cultural development. All of these make Guilin one of the cities in Guangxi which set up foreign affairs organizations at the earliest time and one of the first alternatives for entertaining foreign friends. As a matter of fact, not a few national leaders and government heads make a special trip to Guilin during their state visit. For instance, five American Presidents had visited Guilin during or after their presidency.

For over 40 years, Guilin government has been positively expanding foreign exchange and communication channel. Under the tender care of Vice Chairman Liao Chengzhi, Guilin first established friendly relationship as International Sister Cities with Kumamoto City of Japan in October, 1979. Afterwards, Guilin established friendly relationship as International Sister Cities with cities from New Zealand, America and other countries successively. Guilin and its sister cities make communication and cooperation in economy, culture, education, tourism, environmental protection, science and technology, urban construction and many other fields, not merely promoting the mutual understanding and friendship between Guilin people and people from other countries, but also expanding the cooperation fields between cities. Meanwhile, they strengthen the international influence of Guilin landscape culture and advance the social economic development and civilization progress.

According to the statistics, Guilin has entertained over 150 political leaders, including state leaders and government heads, and goodwill missions and persons from various countries across the world. As a friendship bridge connecting China to the outside world, beautiful Guilin composes a chapter of friendship and peace in new China's foreign exchange stage.

With the development of regional transportation, ethnic contact, cultural and art communication, and contact between people from different strata of society, presenting gifts has become an important content for diplomatic formalities and folk etiquette. During the foreign exchange, political leaders, goodwill missions and persons from various countries across the world have presented numerous precious gifts to Guilin government and leaders. From the 1970s till now, all of the gifts presented by foreign guests have been registered, put into record and turned over to the authorities, and then transferred to Guilin Museum by Foreign Affairs Office of the People's Government of Guilin Municipality for collection. Presently, the number of foreign guest gifts collected by Guilin Museum hits nearly 3,000, which ranks the third in China, secondary only to that of International Friendship Museum and the Military Museum of the Chinese People's Revolution. As one of the Guilin Museum collection resources with distinctive regional characteristics, the gifts have become the quintessence of the friendship between Guilin people and people from other countries, and witness the friendly contact between Guilin people and people from other foreign countries. Demonstrating the great achievement made in Guilin foreign exchange work, the gifts are the window through which we appreciate the exotic culture essence and art style.

Boasting gorgeous color, varied styles and distinctive features, the foreign guest gifts collected by Guilin Museum are of different categories, including gold and silver ware, bronze and iron ware, jade and stone ware, ceramic ware, glassware, lacquer ware, ivory and bone objects, wooden ware, textile goods, painting and photography, all with distinctive regional characteristics. Representing excellent traditional culture and unique art style of various countries, these gifts are of great historical value, art value and memorial and symbolic significance, and vividly reflect the production, living, culture, religion, clothing and folk customs of various nationalities. Fraught with human being's natural and simple creation emotions, every gift is the quintessence of the diligence and wisdom of the people throughout the world. Ancient Grecian poet Pindar once said, "Every gift, despite its size, will be the best gift so long as it contains emotions."

We hereby present the selected nearly 200 foreign guest gifts to readers, expecting the readers could, through appreciating and understanding gifts, appreciate the exotic culture and reveal the eternal theme human beings pursue — peace and progress. We hope the art treasures from afar could bring readers warm friendship and unforgettable art enjoyment.

第一单元　亚洲礼品揽胜

亚洲，是“亚细亚洲”的简称，为世界第一大洲，面积约4400万平方千米，占世界陆地总面积的29.4%。总人口约40亿，约占世界总人口的60.4%，居世界第一位。亚洲是佛教、伊斯兰教和基督教的发源地。

截止至2011年7月31日，有45个亚洲国家与我国建立了外交关系。

亚洲地域广袤，物产丰富，民族众多，文化习俗不尽相同，礼品风格迥异。亚洲国家的礼品，均展示出东方人特有的气质。鎏金漆器上昂首挺胸的金黄圣狮和云纹，带有浓郁的缅甸佛教文化传统和地域特色；装帧精美华贵的《古兰经》，则为伊斯兰教的经典；玉石、小岱烧和各种漆画，体现了亚洲各地文化之间的交流；而那些细腻生动的人形、偶人，均展示出东方人特有的气质。

Chapter 1　Asian Gifts

Asia, short for "Asian continent", is the biggest continent in the world. It covers an area of around 44 million square kilometers, accounting for 29.4% of the world's total land area. The total population is around 4 billion, which takes up 60.4% of the whole world population and ranks the first in the world. Asia is also the origin place of Buddhism, Islam and Christianity.

Till July 3lst, 2011, 45 Asian countries had established diplomatic relations with China.

Asia boasts vast territory, abundant resources, numerous ethnic groups and varied cultural customs, all of which lead to different styles of gifts. Gifts from Asian countries present unique temperament of eastern people. The golden sacred lion and cloud veins on the gilt lacquer ware present profound Burmese Buddhism cultural tradition and regional features; the profusely decorated *Quran* is the classic of Islamism; jade and different kinds of lacquer picture reflect the communication between Asian regional cultures; the fine, vivid figures and puppets demonstrate the unique disposition of eastern people.

001

1976年巴基斯坦学生代表团赠镂雕花卉铜挂盘

直径34.5cm

Bronze Hanging Plate with Openwork of Flowers

Gift of the Student Delegation of Pakistan, 1976

Diameter 34.5cm

002（上）

1983年巴基斯坦总统齐亚·哈克赠绣花皮提包（几何纹）

高20.5cm，宽23.5cm

Leather Handbag with Embroidery of Geometric Patterns

Gift of Muhammad Zia-ul-Haq, the President of Pakistan, 1983

Height 20.5cm, width 23.5cm

003（下）

1983年巴基斯坦总统齐亚·哈克赠绣花皮提包（团花纹）

高20.5cm，宽23.5cm

Leather Handbag with Embroidery of Flowers

Gift of Muhammad Zia-ul-Haq, the President of Pakistan, 1983

Height 20.5cm, width 23.5cm

004

1983年巴基斯坦总统齐亚·哈克赠坐垫套

直径41cm

Round Cushion Cover

Gift of Muhammad Zia-ul-Haq, the President of Pakistan, 1983

Diameter 41cm

005

1983年巴基斯坦总统齐亚·哈克赠花瓶

左：高15.4cm，口径4.9cm，腹径13cm，底长7cm、宽7cm；中：高31cm，口径8.3cm，腹径13.2cm，底径10cm；右：高19.3cm，口径7.1cm，腹径9.4cm，底径8.3cm

Vases

Gift of Muhammad Zia-ul-Haq, the President of Pakistan, 1983

Left: height 15.4cm, diameter of mouth 4.9cm, diameter of belly 13cm, length of base 7cm, width of base 7cm; middle: height 31cm, diameter of mouth 8.3cm, diameter of belly 13.2cm, diameter of base 10cm; right: height 19.3cm, diameter of mouth 7.1cm, diameter of belly 9.4cm, diameter of base 8.3cm

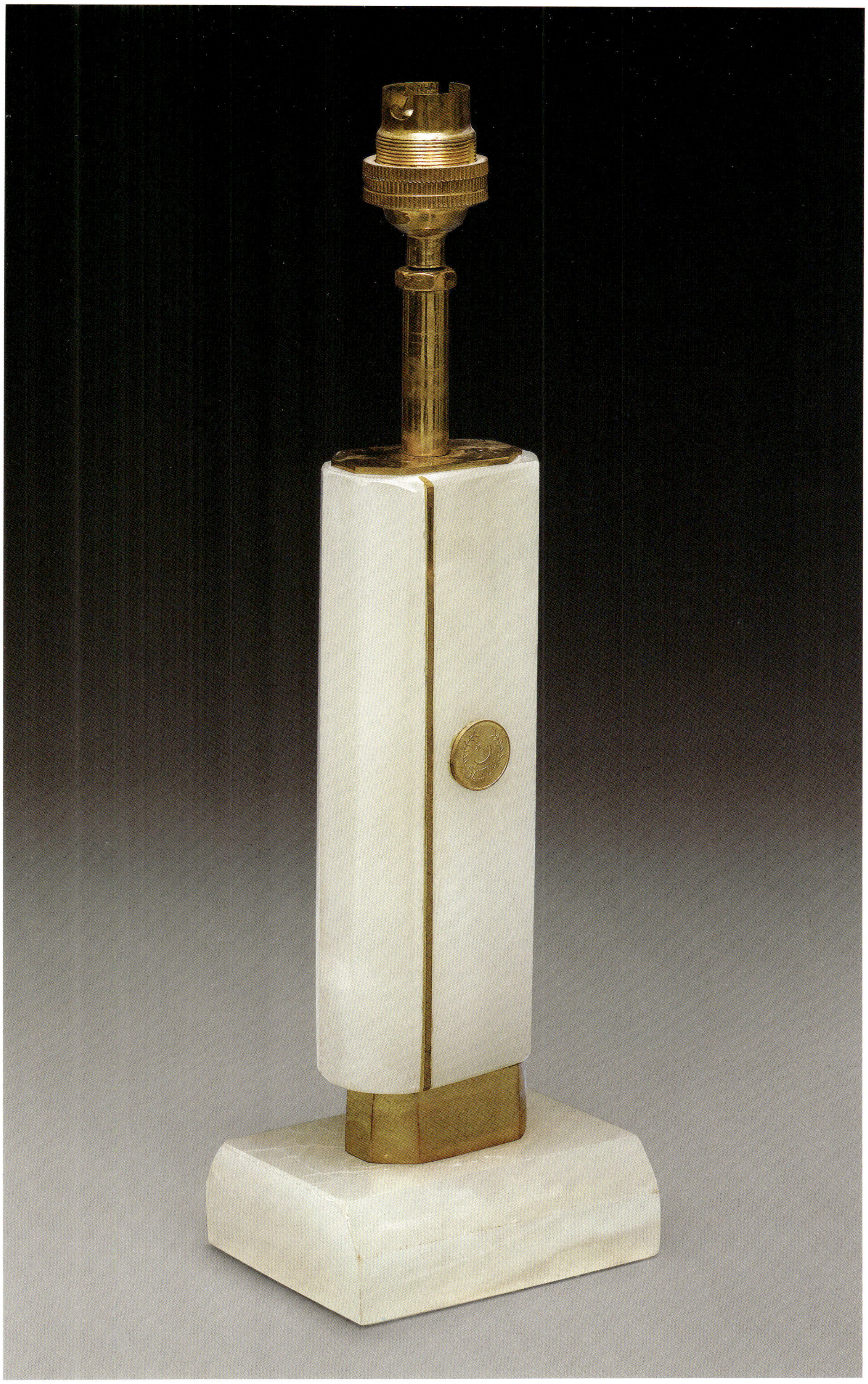

006

1983年巴基斯坦总统齐亚·哈克赠玉台灯座

高35.5cm，宽10cm

Jade Table Lamp Holder

Gift of Muhammad Zia-ul-Haq, the President of Pakistan, 1983

Height 35.5cm, width10cm

007

1983年巴基斯坦总统齐亚・哈克赠玉盒

通高7.5cm，腹径11.3cm，足高0.5cm

Jade Box

Gift of Muhammad Zia-ul-Haq, the President of Pakistan, 1983

Overall height 7.5cm, diameter of belly 11.3cm, height of foot 0.5cm

008

1983年巴基斯坦总统齐亚·哈克赠红木盒

高3.7cm，口径19.3cm，腹径20.4cm

Rosewood Box

Gift of Muhammad Zia-ul-Haq, the President of Pakistan, 1983

Height 3.7cm, diameter of mouth 19.3cm, diameter of belly 20.4cm

009（上）

1984年巴基斯坦工业部长赠牧羊图毛织挂毯

高64cm，宽90cm

Knitwear Tapestry with Design of Shepherding

Gift of the Industry Minister of Pakistan, 1984

Height 64cm, width 90cm

010（下）

1984年巴基斯坦工业部长赠织锦挂毯

高92cm，宽160cm

Tapestry

Gift of the Industry Minister of Pakistan, 1984

Height 92cm, width 160cm

011

1984年巴基斯坦工业部长赠舞姬挂毯

高108cm，宽29cm

Tapestry with Design of Dancers

Gift of the Industry Minister of Pakistan, 1984

Height 108cm, width 29cm

012

1984年巴基斯坦工业部长赠狩猎图挂毯

高98cm，宽28.8cm

Tapestry with Design of Hunting

Gift of the Industry Minister of Pakistan, 1984

Height 98cm, width 28.8cm

013（上）

1984年巴基斯坦工业部长赠浮雕缠枝花银盘

直径15.5cm

Silver Plate with Relief Decoration of Floral Scrolls

Gift of the Industry Minister of Pakistan, 1984

Diameter 15.5cm

014（下）

1984年巴基斯坦工业部长赠浮雕独立塔银盘

直径20.1cm

Silver Plate with Relief Decoration of Minar-E-Pakistan

Gift of the Industry Minister of Pakistan, 1984

Diameter 20.1cm

015（上）

1984年巴基斯坦工业部长赠金丝绒盘花坐垫

高29cm，宽33cm

Pleuche Cushion with Design of Scrolled Flowers

Gift of the Industry Minister of Pakistan, 1984

Height 29cm, width 33cm

016（下）

1984年巴基斯坦文官学院赠鎏金鱼鸟纹铜盘

高1.3cm，直径20.1cm

Bronze Plate with Gilded Design of Fish and Birds

Gift of the Civil Service College of Pakistan, 1984

Height 1.3cm, diameter 20.1cm

017

1998年巴基斯坦国民议会议长卜克·苏姆罗赠玉石台灯

通高20.1cm，底径13.4cm

Jade Table Lamp

Gift of Elahi Bux Soomro, the Speaker of National Assembly of Pakistan, 1998

Overall height 20.1cm, diameter of base 13.4cm

018

1976年朝鲜友人赠瓷猫头鹰

通高15cm

Porcelain Owl

Gift of North Korean Friends, 1976

Overall height 15cm

019

1977年朝鲜劳动党友好参观团赠歌舞瓷人

通高25.5cm、20.5cm

Porcelain Dancers

Gift of the Touring Party of the Workers' Party of North Korea, 1977

Overall height 25.5cm, 20.5cm

这三尊美人瓷像，头部小巧玲珑，两手平腰托着吊钟花，挽住遮盖着下身的衣衫，感觉和维纳斯像一样，呈现出一种静止和严肃的美。

她们来自美丽的金刚山，传说也十分动人。相传远古时代，有个猎人正在追赶一只梅花鹿。一个青年樵夫见小鹿可怜，便把它藏在自己积攒的柴禾里。小鹿为了报恩，来到樵夫家中，见他仍没有妻子，便跟他说："天上有八位仙女，每天到要下八潭来洗澡。洗澡的时候，她们会脱下身上的轻纱，你如果偷偷把谁的轻纱收起来，她就回不去了。你何不选一位仙女作自己的妻子呢？"樵夫听了小鹿的话，找了个机会，拿走其中最年轻仙女的轻纱。樵夫和仙女成了亲，不久还有了孩子，过着美满的生活。一次，樵夫出于好心，把轻纱还给了仙女，这下勾起了仙女对七位姐姐的思念，于是带着孩子回娘家探亲去了。樵夫打柴回来，不见自己的妻儿，悲痛万分。这下小鹿又跑回来给他献计，说那次众仙女下凡洗澡的事触怒了玉皇，严禁仙女再次下凡，但允许她们每天从天上将吊桶吊下来取水。小鹿让樵夫设法爬进吊桶。樵夫听了小鹿的话，上了天，同玉皇进行了一场斗争，把妻儿接回了美丽的金刚山。据说，后面七位仙女因羡慕他们的幸福生活，也飞到了金刚山。金刚山地下的金、钨等宝藏都是她们埋的，许多珍禽奇兽也是她们饲养的，还有许多金钱菊、吊钟花等植物也是她们培植的。这样奇妙的传说还很多，反映了朝鲜人民对美好生活的憧憬，以八仙女下金刚山为题材的工艺品也比比皆是。

这三尊美人瓷像，就是金刚山上八仙女中的三位，两尊右手高举她们亲手种植的金灯笼花，另一尊平腰托着吊钟花，象征着清洁与谦虚。这三位行动婀娜、宛如飘飞的仙女到桂林，这大概是对甲天下的桂林山水慕名而来了。

020（上）

1981年朝鲜劳动党友好参观团赠双层瓷花瓶

高13.7cm，口径3.9cm

Double-layer Porcelain Vase

Gift of the Touring Group of the Workers' Party of North Korea, 1981

Overall height 13.7cm, diameter of mouth 3.9cm

021（下）

1992年朝鲜中朝边境检查团赠豆青釉镂雕花卉瓷瓶

高22.9cm，口径9.5cm，腹径14cm

Pea-green Glazed Vase with Openwork of Flowers

Gift of the Inspection Team of China–North Korea Border of North Korea, 1992

Height 22.9cm, diameter of mouth 9.5cm, diameter of belly 14cm

022

1988年朝鲜对外文委代表团赠蓝釉茶具

盘：高1.7cm，直径6.3cm；杯：高2.9cm，口径5.6 cm；壶：通高8cm

Blue-glazed Tea Set

Gift of the Delegation of Committee for Cultural Relations with Foreign Countries of North Korea, 1988

Plate: height 1.7cm, diameter 6.3cm; cup: height 2.9cm, diameter of mouth 5.6cm; teapot: overall height 8cm

023（上）

1978年菲律宾青年友协观光团赠日历笔架

高5.9cm，宽25.7cm

Penholders with Calendar

Gift of the Touring Group of Youth Travel Association of Philippines, 1978

Height 5.9cm, width 25.7cm

024（下）

1980年菲律宾农业代表团赠椰树小屋鹿角雕

高13.8cm，宽12.5cm

Antler Sculpture of Coconut Tree and House

Gift of the Agriculture Delegation of Philippines, 1980

Height 13.8cm, width 12.5cm

025（上）

1993年哈萨克斯坦大学校长萨迪科夫赠毛呢帽

高28.5cm，宽38.5cm

Woolen Hat

Gift of Sadikov, the President of University of Kazakhstan, 1993

Height 28.5cm, width 38.5cm

026（下）

1993年哈萨克斯坦大学校长萨迪科夫赠军绿长袍

衣长128cm，袖长66cm，胸围128cm，腰带长169cm

Army Green Robe

Gift of Sadikov, the President of University of Kazakhstan, 1993

Length 128cm, length of sleeve 66cm, chest 128cm, length of belt 169cm

027

1992年韩国工商部代表团赠寿挂牌

通高108cm，直径20.5cm

Pendant with Character "*shou* (longevity)" on Tassels

Gift of the Delegation of Ministry of Industry and Commerce of Korea, 1992

Overall height 108cm, diameter 20.5cm

028（上）

1996年韩国济州代表团赠木雕“背水的济州姑娘”

基座：长24cm，宽17cm，高3cm；通高36cm

Wood Carving of a Cheju Girl Carrying a Water Basket on the Back

Gift of the Delegation of Cheju, Korea, 1996

Base: length 24cm, width 17cm, height 3cm; overall height 36cm

029（下）

韩国济州市议会长姜英彻赠济州风光纪念盘

高1.1cm，长径34cm，短径28cm

Plate Emblazoned with Scenery of Cheju

Gift of Jiang Yingche, the Mayor of Cheju, Korea

Height 1.1cm, major axis 34cm, minor axis 28cm

030

1996年韩国釜山议会代表团赠百济金铜香炉

通高27cm，口径8.8cm，底径11.4cm

Replica of Gilded-bronze Incense Burner of Baekje

Gift of the Delegation of Busan Council, Korea, 1996

Overall height 27cm, diameter of mouth 8.8cm, diameter of base 11.4cm

百济金铜大香炉，高64厘米，直径19厘米，重11.8千克，制作于公元6世纪，是百济和韩国传统文化的经典之作。香炉1993年出土于百济王室寺庙——扶余陵山里寺庙遗址，以其绚丽多姿的造型、精湛的铸造工艺、多元的文化内涵，给世界带来不小的震动。据推测，该香炉可能是用于王室仪礼的仪典明器。1996年5月30日香炉被指定为大韩民国第287号国宝，现藏于韩国国立扶余博物馆。这是其仿制品。

金铜大香炉由香炉盖、炉身、底座组成。香炉盖顶部刻着凤凰，下面有五位乐师在演奏乐器。74座山峰上刻着大树、岩石、溪水及瀑布，还刻着老虎、鹿、大象、猴子等42只动物和6种植物、12个人物。炉盖共设有12个隐蔽的出烟孔，顶部凤凰的胸脯上有2个，围绕着山峰有10个，点燃香火时，烟雾如同雾霭缕缕升起。香碗，也就是炉身，由三层莲瓣相互交错构成，每片莲瓣及莲瓣之间雕有人物、迦陵频伽、鹿、鹤、鱼等各式图样。底座上雕有一条曲颈躬身、腾飞起舞的龙。香炉盖寓意大地，炉身和底座寓意着水，其基本思想源于阴阳原理。

体现出神仙、莲花等道教和佛教综合特点的金铜大香炉可以说是百济人精神世界和艺术世界的集合。

031

济州市长高玟洙赠多尔哈鲁邦石雕像

高30.5cm，宽24.5cm

Dolharubang

Gift of Gao Wenzhu, the Mayor of Cheju, Korea

Height 30.5cm, width 24.5cm

济州的象征物——多尔哈鲁邦（石头公公）。在今天，济州岛不再是地处边陲的小岛。多尔哈鲁邦作为济州的象征物，也正在向全世界宣扬其名声。多尔哈鲁邦，韩语就是“石头公公”的意思。这些石像，原来并不叫多尔哈鲁邦，但因为好记、容易称呼，道民开始称其为多尔哈鲁邦而流传开来。多尔哈鲁邦的名称真正得到确定，是在1971年8月26日，济州道文化财委员会在制定民俗资料时，在一番讨论之后，决定以“多尔哈鲁邦”为该文化财的正式名称。

根据学者的考证，多尔哈鲁邦从前有翁仲石、望柱石等称呼（其意义与图腾相近）。遗留下来的真品多尔哈鲁邦目前得到确认的有两尊在首尔景福宫，济州岛内还保存有47尊，模样稍有不同。济州多尔哈鲁邦石像是济州岛的守护神，以熔岩石制成，也称为“忧石木”、“模石木”、“卜首”等。济州岛村庄入口处可以看到压低帽子的石像，立在城门外，有咒术、禁标的功能。而作为村庄的守护神、地区间的界标和路标的雕像则立在村口。

032（上）

1983年马来西亚政府代表团赠浮雕猪纪念盘

直径20.4cm

Plate with Relief Decoration of a Pig

Gift of the Delegation of Malaysia Government, 1983

Diameter 20.4cm

033（中、下）

1983年马来西亚政府代表团赠浮雕农事图纪念盘

直径12.6cm

Plates with Relief Decoration of Agricultural Activity

Gift of the Delegation of Malaysia Government, 1983

Diameter 12.6cm

034

1977年孟加拉友人赠银质熏香用具

左：高5.9cm，腹径4.5cm；中：高5.1cm，口径2.1cm，底径2.8cm；

右：高6.1cm，腹径4.6cm

Silver Incense Articles

Gift of Friends from Bangladesh, 1977

Left: height 5.9cm, diameter of belly 4.5cm; middle: height 5.1cm, diameter of mouth 2.1cm, diameter of base 2.8cm; right: height 6.1cm, diameter of belly 4.6cm

035（上）

1977年缅甸吴奈温总统赠贝壳圆盒

高5.5cm，直径12cm

Cylindrical Boxes Made of Shells

Gift of Ne Win, the President of Burma, 1977

Height 5.5cm, diameter 12cm

036（下）

1977年缅甸吴奈温总统赠鎏金茶叶盒

通高11cm，直径8cm

Gilded Tea Box

Gift of Ne Win, the President of Burma, 1977

Overall height 11cm, diameter 8cm

037

1977年缅甸吴奈温总统赠鎏金柚木漆果盒

通高6.5cm，直径25.5cm

Gilded Teak Fruit-box Coated With Lacquer

Gift of Ne Win, the President of Burma, 1977

Overall height 6.5cm, diameter 25.5cm

缅甸的漆器制作起源于12至13世纪的蒲甘，自此之后，蒲甘便成为缅甸乃至东南亚地区的漆器发源地之一，是东南亚最富盛名的漆器之乡。

这里的竹漆器工艺品大多数是手工制造，物美价廉。漆器的生产周期需要数月的时间，那圆形的器皿都是用削得细细的竹片一圈圈环绕编制而成的，大致的工艺过程包括用马尾制泥胎、反复上漆、自然风干、雕刻、套色绘制等。上漆的遍数和设计颜色的丰富与否，以及颜料的不同基质，决定着漆器的等级和价格。作为日常用品和馈赠礼品，古代包括缅族人在内的缅甸人喜欢全家在一个带底座的漆器大圆盘中吃饭，用漆器水杯喝水，认为用漆器餐具吃饭更香甜，用漆器水杯喝水更清凉。

蒲甘出产的漆器表面上通常绘有各种图案，大致有四种：带有镀金花纹的黑色漆器、暗红色漆器、带有凸起镀金图案的漆器和全部镀金的漆器。在蒲甘艺人眼里，一件件精美的漆器就如同蒲甘两千多座佛塔一样，千姿百态，别具一格。这些漆器上描绘着圣狮和云纹的图案，充满浓郁的佛教色彩。缅甸是信奉佛教的国家，云纹表示缅甸是一个幸福极乐的天国；狮子是佛教的吉祥物，被誉为缅甸的国兽，称圣狮，是吉祥的标志。

038

1977年缅甸吴奈温总统赠鎏金柚木漆套盘

外层：高4.1cm，口径21.4cm，腹径25.3cm；中层：高3.7cm，口径17cm，腹径20cm；内层：高3.1cm，口径13.1cm，腹径15.6cm

Nested Gilded Teak Plates Coated with Lacquer

Gift of Ne Win, the President of Burma, 1977

The outermost plate: height 4.1cm, diameter of mouth 21.4cm, diameter of belly 25.3cm;
the middle plate: height 3.7cm, diameter of mouth 17cm, diameter of belly 20cm;
the innermost plate: height 3.1cm, diameter of mouth 13.1cm, diameter of belly 15.6cm

039

1995年缅甸外交部副部长赠"桑柯"弯琴

通高55.5cm，船高45.5cm，宽52cm

Saung-Gauk (curving *Qin*)

Gift of the Vice Foreign Minister of Burma, 1995

Overall height 55.5cm, height of ship 45.5cm, width 52cm

这是缅甸最主要的民族乐器（缅语为"桑柯"），是缅甸所特有的弓形竖琴，我国唐朝时称它为凤首箜篌。弯琴的外形很美，高高耸起的弯曲琴颈顶端的金叶是菩提树叶的象征。它的共鸣体是用一块木头雕成的，形状像一条船，上面蒙上一块红色的鹿皮，四周饰以金色的波浪形花纹，再加上飘舞在琴颈上的红色饰带和穗子，使乐器显得十分雍容华贵、精致典雅。弯琴的琴弦一般有13根至16根，按五声音阶定音。音乐家将琴放在腿上、抱在胸前演奏，音色清新雅致，娓娓动听。它最早的用途是为歌唱伴奏，现在常独奏或与其他乐器合奏。

其实弯琴本来不是缅甸乐器，它起源于古埃及或美索不达米亚，经过阿拉伯、伊朗、印度（或印度尼西亚）传入缅甸；如今其他地方都已失传，只在缅甸得以保存并得到发展，不得不说是一个奇迹。而缅甸弯琴，正是古代乐器中的一件活化石。今天弯琴在外来文化的冲击下仍然十分活跃，有时还与小提琴和围鼓合奏，既保持自己的风格，又获得了新的生命力。

040

1976年尼泊尔元帅尼尔赠镶嵌铜独角犀牛

高6.2cm，长8.5cm

Bronze One-horned Rhinoceros Decorated with Inlay

Gift of the Marshal of Nepal, 1976

Height 6.2cm, length 8.5cm

尼泊尔奇特旺皇家国家公园，1973年被联合国教科文组织列为世界文化遗产。那里生活着珍贵的稀有动物——独角犀牛，是世界上濒临灭绝的动物，现全球仅存2000余头。

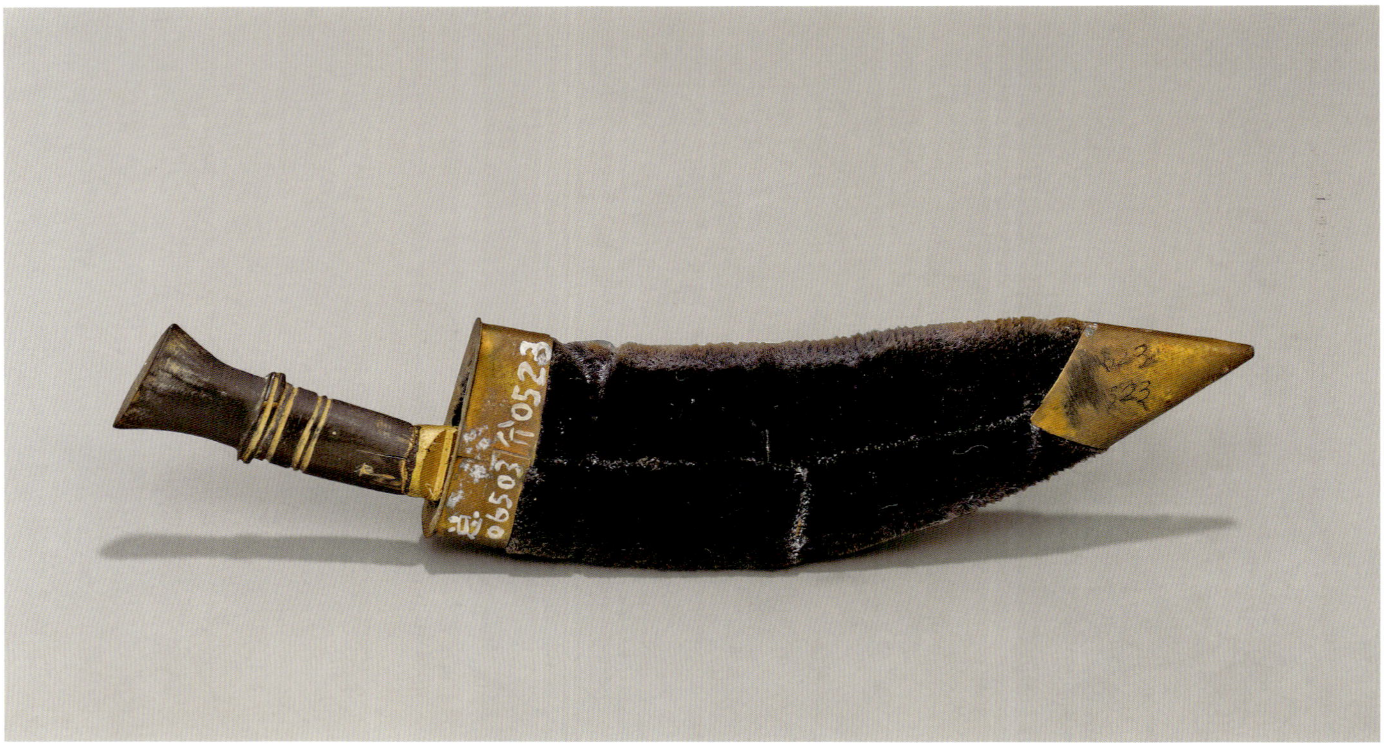

041（上）

1978年尼泊尔教授赠掐丝铜盒

高2.6cm，直径4.8cm

Bronze Box Decorated with Wire Inlay

Gift of a Professor from Nepal, 1978

Height2.6cm, diameter 4.8cm

042（下）

1978年尼泊尔教授赠铜刀

长14.9cm，通宽3cm

Bronze Knife

Gift of a Professor from Nepal, 1978

Length 14.9cm, overall width 3cm

043

1993年尼泊尔国王赠巴德岗木雕

高41.2cm，通宽35.5cm

Bhadgaon Wood Carving

Gift of the King of Nepal, 1993

Height 41.2cm, overall width 35.5cm

044

1993年尼泊尔国王赠浮雕塔莱珠女神庙镀银盘

高0.8cm，长径13cm，短径10.5cm

Silvering Plate with Relief Decoration of Taleju Tample

Gift of the King of Nepal, 1993

Height 0.8cm, major axis 13cm, minor axis 10.5cm

045

1978年日本姬路市各界友好访华团赠御矢车

通高162cm，风车轮径59cm

Windmill

Gift of the Visiting Group of Himeji, Japan, 1978

Overall height 162cm, diameter of wheel 59cm

046

1978年日本大阪市议会代表团赠花果水晶玻璃瓶
高20.5cm，口径12.8cm

Crystal Glassware Pot with Design of Flowers and Fruit
Gift of the Delegation of Osaka Council, Japan, 1978
Height 20.5cm, diameter of mouth 12.8cm

047

1980年日本熊本市赠熊本城贴金工艺挂屏

高33cm，宽31.4cm

Hanging Panel of Gilded Kumamoto City

Gift of Kumamoto, Japan, 1980

Height 33cm, width 31.4cm

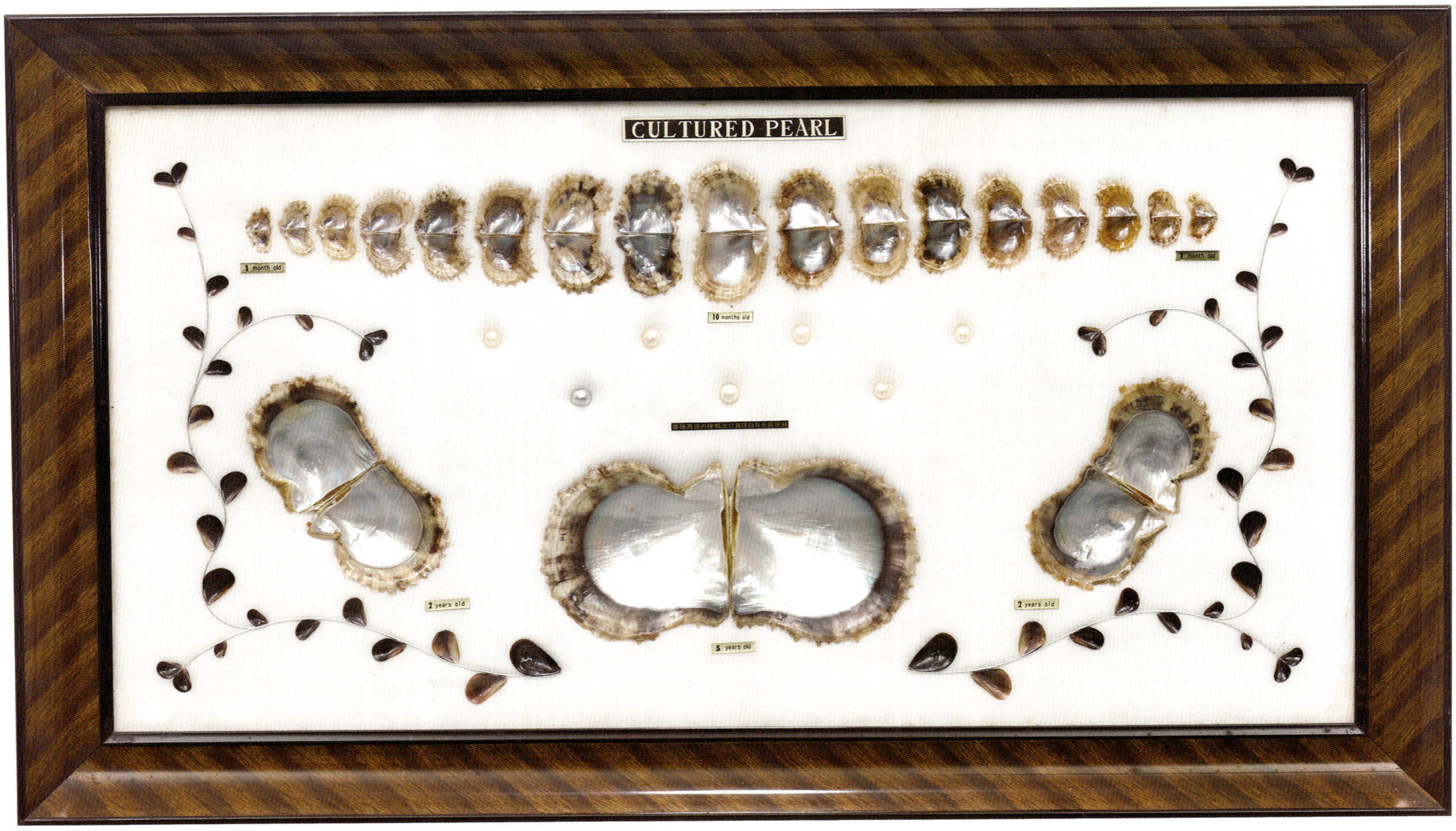

048

1980年日本熊本市友好团赠嵌贝珠工艺挂屏

高37.2cm，宽64cm

Hanging Panel Inlaid with Cultured Pearl

Gift of the Delegation of Kumamoto, Japan, 1980

Height 37.2cm, width 64cm

049

1980年日本熊本市赠博多人形

高39.5cm

Hakata Statue

Gift of Kumamoto, Japan, 1980

Height 39.5cm

博多人形是九州博多的特产，其特点是用粘土烧制成陶，在素陶面上添涂色彩，采用写实的手法，优雅的曲线和丰富细致的表情形成博多人形独特的风格。博多人形被日本指定为传统工艺品。

050

1982年日本盘城代表团赠包金开运不倒翁

高4.4cm，腹径4.3cm

Gilded Bodhidharma Tumbler

Gift of the Delegation of Iwaki, Japan, 1982

Height 4.4cm, diameter of belly 4.3cm

达摩不倒翁，模仿佛教的菩提达摩大师（禅宗始祖）坐禅时的姿态，是日本百姓过年时常用的吉祥饰物，又叫开运福。

051

1983年日本熊本高校生代表团赠鎏金印盒

高5.8cm，直径6.4cm

Gilded Seal Vermilion Box

Gift of the Delegation of Colleges and Universities of Kumamoto, Japan, 1983

Height 5.8cm, diameter 6.4cm

052

1984年日本熊本市高中生团赠仙鹤瓷板画挂屏

高37.7cm，宽30.9cm

Porcelain Hanging Panel with Design of Cranes

Gift of the Delegation of Senior High School of Kumamoto, Japan, 1984

Height 37.7cm, width 30.9cm

053

1984年日本岐阜市访华团赠彩绘花鸟屏风

高92cm，宽181cm

Screen Painted with Flowers and Birds

Gift of the Visiting Group of Gifu, Japan, 1984

Height 92cm, width 181cm

054

1984年日本社长联代表团赠蔬果木盘

直径39.2cm

Wood Plate with Design of Vegetables

Gift of the Delegation of President Union, Japan, 1984

Diameter 39.2cm

箱根木雕画是日本著名的木制镶嵌传统工艺品，早在奈良时期就已成为一项宝贵的技艺，以制作工艺考究而闻名。在制作这种木雕时，首先要选择各种花纹的木材，然后一块一块地反复加工，最后再把加工好的材料镶嵌在一起，组成融艺术、趣味为一体，具有浓郁地方特色的民间工艺品。箱根木雕在日本国内外都受到普遍的欢迎。

055

1985年日本熊本友好之翼访问团赠山鹿灯笼

高34cm

Yamaga Lantern

Gift of the Wings of Friendship Delegation of Kumamoto, Japan, 1985

Height 34cm

山鹿灯笼祭是熊本三大火节之一，在每年夏季八月，山鹿温泉到处悬挂点亮的灯笼，身穿和服的妇女头顶灯笼翩翩起舞。山鹿灯笼的柱和梁都是空洞，别名“无骨灯笼”。

056

1985年熊本友人赠“桐之舞”持扇人形

高41cm

Statue of a Geisha Girl Holding a Fan

Gift of Friends from Kumamoto, Japan, 1985

Height 41cm

日本的人形艺术（又叫偶人），传承自江户时代的玩偶技艺，起源于孩子的玩具，逐渐发展成为深受日本人民喜爱的一门艺术形式。人形种类繁多，制作材料有泥、纸、布、绢、木、竹等。偶人的形象多取材于日本古典艺术形式的舞跃人形和节庆祭祀人形等，内容有反映日本民俗的正月人形、女孩节雏人形、男孩节五月人形等。这些人形恬静优雅、华丽精致，从一个侧面展现了日本历史、文化、民俗的发展历程。

人形美术是日本的一种传统民间美术，有些像中国的绢人，大约起源于日本的江户时代，最早是作为孩子的玩具出现的。经过数百年的发展变化，人形美术以其精巧的造型、华丽的服装和多样的发饰赢得了人们的赞赏，成为日本人民喜爱的一种室内装饰品。在日本人形中，三月人形和五月人形最有代表性，产销量也最多。每年三月女孩节前后，商店里的古装人偶备受青睐。据说这种人偶全国每年出售额达1000亿元左右。

日本父母通过祭祀人偶，表达对女儿的美好心愿。3月3日，母亲娘家的亲属要向女孩赠送“内裹雏”(古装偶人)，女孩家里还在特设的人偶祭坛前摆上桃花、菱形黏糕和白酒。日本人认为孩子如有灾难、病患可以传给偶人，从而使孩子身体健康、成长顺利。人偶祭坛呈阶梯形，上铺红地毯或红布，层数因家庭境况即人偶多少而不同，少则两三层，多则七八层，人偶中有王与后、宫女、大臣、乐队、听差等，还有一些镀金上漆、富丽堂皇的车马、行李、家具、娱乐用品的模型。人偶个个倩笑盼目、栩栩如生。祭祀人偶始于江户时代，当时人偶是纸制的，随着这一风俗的形成，后来出现了布制人偶。到了明治时代，人偶商品化，女孩节祭祀人偶在全国固定下来。

五月人形的由来和端午节有关。在古代日本，每逢五月初五，人们都要举行祈祷平安的节会。参加节会的朝廷官吏们，将据说能驱邪祛病的菖蒲（一种药草）插在冠上，并饮菖蒲酒。在日语中，菖蒲和尚武发音相同，久而久之，五月初五就演变成习武的节日。平安时代，这一天要举行射箭表演。到了江户幕府时期，家家户户则在门前装饰军旗和军马的标志，以后又演变为摆设武士人形。

到了现代，日本政府把五月五日定为“男孩节”。每年这一天，为了祝愿男孩子健康成长，父母们一般都要为一周岁的男孩购买五月人形来摆设，主要是象征男子汉的强壮和勇敢。五月人形一般由武士盔甲、弓箭、剑、鼓和旌旗等组成，有的还有八音盒。人形的服装绚丽多彩，反映了日本传统的服饰文化，令人赏心悦目。

在日本，持扇人形也很多。持扇人形表现了秀丽端庄的少女，她梳着高贵典雅的传统发饰，和服上绣着飞翔的仙鹤，还持一把绘有梅花的折扇，寄寓着美好的祝福。

057

1986年日本福冈市代表团赠鲤鱼旗

通高157cm，旗最长140cm，帆长145cm

Carp Windsocks

Gift of the Delegation of Fukuoka, Japan, 1986

Overall height 157cm, the maximum length of flag 140cm, length of sail 145cm

五月五日是日本男孩节，这天有男孩的家庭都要悬挂鲤鱼旗，插菖蒲叶，设置兜铠和弓箭，装饰五月人形，吃去邪的糕团（称"柏饼"）或粽子。鲤鱼旗一般从上到下依次挂上燕尾旗（河流）、黑鲤鱼（父亲）、红鲤鱼（母亲）及小鲤鱼，小鲤鱼的数目就是家中男孩的数目。鲤鱼勇敢顽强，不怕惊涛骇浪，用它来祝贺男孩，意在激励男孩在人生的征途上，能像鲤鱼那样不畏艰难险阻，勇于逆流而上，一往直前。男孩节源于中国的端午节，现在成为日本五大传统节日之一，为全国公休日。

058（上）

1985年日本友人赠黄釉彩绘瓷盘

高3.7cm，直径24.7cm

Yellow-glazed Porcelain Plate Decorated with Colored Drawings

Gift of Japanese Friends

Height 3.7cm, diameter 24.7cm

059（下）

1986年熊本青年文化交流访问团赠山水人物五彩瓷盘

高5cm，直径36.5cm

Porcelain Plate Decorated with Polychrome Design of Landscape and Figures

Gift of the Visiting Group of Youth Culture Exchange of Kumamoto, Japan, 1986

Height 5cm, diameter 36.5cm

060

1988年日本第二回善邻访中团赠五彩瓷罐

罐：高19.5cm，口径10.7cm，腹径19cm；车：通高28.3cm，长39cm，宽20.7cm

Porcelain Jar with Overglaze Polychrome Design

Gift of the second Friendly Visiting Group from Japan, 1988

Jar: height 19.5cm, diameter of mouth 10.7cm, diameter of belly 19cm; cart: overall height 28.3cm, length 39cm, width 20.7cm

九谷烧，日式彩绘瓷器，因发祥地九谷而得名，距今已有350年的历史，世界名瓷之一。日本的彩绘瓷器从中国彩绘系统发展而来，但经过本土工匠的刻苦钻研，结合日本固有的风土人情，最终形成自己独特的彩绘风格。

九谷烧瓷器风格高雅、技艺独特，善于采用金、银等贵重材料进行装饰或绘画，绘画线条明快，色彩鲜艳，老的九谷烧有绿、黄、红、紫、藏青色等五种颜色。九谷烧至今全程手工制作，共有14道工序，常作为对外交往的馈赠礼品。

061

1988年日本鸟羽市代表团赠贝壳帆船

通高33.4cm，通宽38.5cm

Shell Sailboat

Gift of the Delegation of Toba, Japan, 1988

Overall height 33.4cm, overall width 38.5cm

062

1988年日本鸟羽市代表团赠嵌珍珠贝壳画

高31.2cm，横37.8cm，厚4.6cm

Shell and Pearl Inlay Work (crane)

Gift of the Delegation of Toba, Japan, 1988

Height 31.2cm, width 37.8cm, thickness 4.6cm

063

1989年日本相模原市第14次使节团赠宝石镶嵌梅花图挂画

高46cm，宽55cm，厚6.5cm

Hanging Picture of Plum Blossoms Inlaid with Jewels

Gift of the 14th Envoy Delegation of Sagamihara, Japan, 1989

Height 46cm, width 55cm, thickness 6.5cm

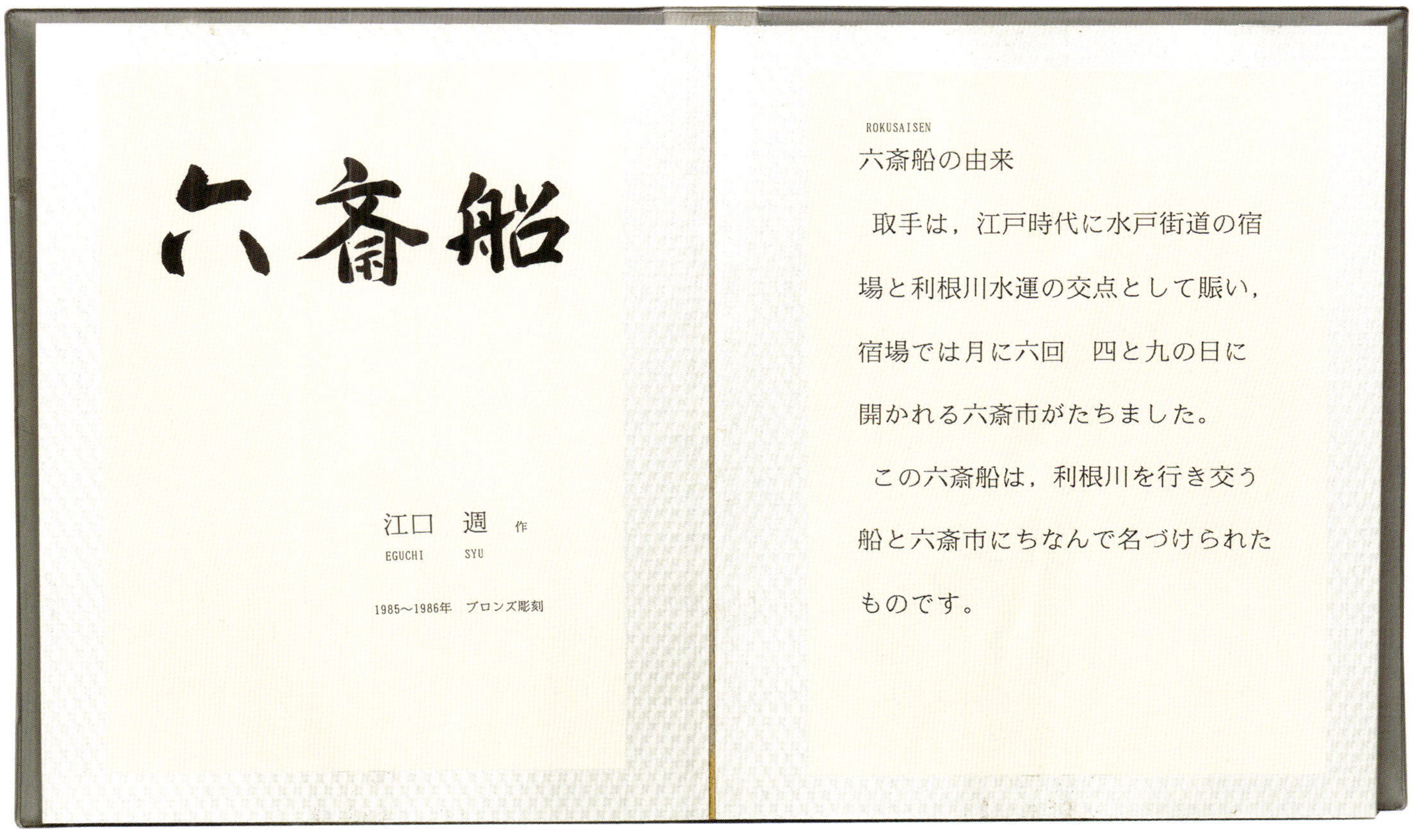

064

1990年日本取手市市长菊地胜志郎赠铸铁六斋船模型（附说明书）

通高23.5cm，长42.5cm，宽17cm

Liuzhai Ship Model (including instruction)

Gift of Kikuchi Katsushirō, the Mayor of Toride, Japan, 1990

Overall height 23.5cm, length 42.5cm, width 17cm

065

1990年日本取手市议会代表团赠御押绘羽子板饰

高54.5cm，宽21cm

Hagoita (traditional Japanese craft)

Gift of the Delegation of the Council of Toride, Japan, 1990

Height 54.5cm, width 21cm

羽子板是日本传统中长方形有花样的木板，类似现今的羽毛球拍，产生于日本室町时代。分为比赛板羽球用的羽子板和装饰艺术用的羽子板。板羽球（日语：羽根突き），常中译作羽球，但其实与羽球不同，是一种日本传统上在新年时主要为女孩玩的游戏或运动，两人以羽子板互相打击毽子（羽根），让毽子掉落的一方就输了，输的一方被在脸上涂墨作为处罚。

当初只作为拍羽根突的工具，在天皇的宫中，由公卿和宫女们分成两组进行。后来人们认为它可以慢慢祓除不祥，板羽球成为正月女性的避邪习俗，传说是古代西王母的化身。进入江户时代的时候，“押绘羽子板”开始流行，仿照了歌舞伎演员的造型，现代被指定为东京的传统工艺品，现在也有仿照现代名人样貌的作品。羽子板上的彩色图案华丽、讲究，采用浮世绘和贴画等传统工艺制作，色彩斑斓，精美无比，成为日本百姓喜欢的工艺品和玩具。

066

1990年日本冲绳市长会代表团赠牡丹漆画盘

直径36.5cm

Lacquer Plate Painted with Ponies

Gift of the Delegation of the Mayor Association of Okinawa, Japan, 1990

Diameter 36.5cm

067

1991年日本茨城县第一次访中团赠奈良法起寺三重塔木雕模型

通高32cm，长12.5cm，宽12.2cm

Wood Model of Three-stored Pagoda of Hokki-ji

Gif of the first Visiting Group of Ibaraki-ken, Japan, 1991

Overall height 32cm, length 12.5cm, width 12.2cm

法起寺三重塔位于奈良县斑鸠町，属于日本国宝级文物，不仅是日本国内最古老的佛塔，也是日本仅次于药师寺东塔的第二大三重塔，高约24米。法起寺创建于638年，据说是山背大兄王将圣德太子的冈本宫改建而成的，江户时代的建筑物中只剩下了706年完工的三重塔。现法起寺已被列入世界文化遗产名录。比起香火旺盛的法隆寺，法起寺显得清净许多，结构简单朴素的木造三重塔静静地伫立着，与周围宁静的田园风景融为一体，带给人无限的庄重和怀旧感。

068

1991年日本加古川市友好访问团赠日本金箔细工工艺风景屏风

通高26.8cm，宽33.5cm，厚2.3cm

Screen with Design of Sailing among Snow Mountains (Japanese gold foil craft)

Gift of the Visiting Group of Kakogawa, Japan, 1991

Overall height 26.8cm, width 33.5cm, thickness 2.3cm

069

1991年日本加古川市友好访问团赠金箔细工菊花纹插花壶

通高19.4cm，宽20cm，口径6cm，厚9.3cm

Pot with Gilded Design of Chrysanthemums, for Arranging Flowers (Japanese gold foil craft)

Gift of the Visiting Group of Kakogawa, Japan, 1991

Overall height 19.4cm, width 20cm, diameter of mouth 6cm, thickness 9.3cm

日本加古川的金箔工艺，其金箔的厚度仅为万分之一厘米到千分之一厘米，金箔表面闪耀着特殊的金色光辉。

070

1991年日本岩手县南部议会访问团赠铸铁提梁壶

通高19cm，壶高11cm，口径8.5cm，腰围52cm，底径9cm

Loop-handled Iron Teapot

Gift of the Visiting Group of the Southern Council of Iwate-ken, Japan, 1991

Overall height 19cm, height of teapot 11cm, diameter of mouth 8.5cm, perimeter of belly 52cm, diameter of base 9cm

071

1991年日本取手市议会议员吉田一生赠日本和服女装

长190cm

Female Type Kimono

Gift of Yoshida, Member of Totte Council, Japan, 1991

Length 190cm

和服是日本独特的传统服装，于奈良时代从中国唐代传入，首先在贵族中流行，称“唐风贵族服”。平安时代不断演变改进，成为日本国服。它宽大舒适，端庄典雅，特别是女式和服，色彩和花纹鲜艳夺目，由十余种附件组成，且不同的和服配不同的发型，腰带的结法也有变化。女人穿上和服就构成一幅美丽的图画，每个举动都变换出另一幅画面。因此和服既是生活中的实用品，又是一种颇具欣赏价值的艺术品。女式和服的款式和花色之差是区别年龄与婚否的标志。例如，未婚姑娘穿红领衬衣、宽袖外服，已婚妇女着素色衬衣、紧袖外服。腰带是女式和服极为重要的部分，上面刺绣着美丽的花纹图案。它起初窄而细，只起固定作用，后发展为装饰品，到江户末期竟达9寸宽、1.2丈长。腰带的结法很多，其中“大鼓结”比较广泛，即在后腰打结处的腰带内垫一个用纸或布做的芯子，看上去像个方盒。

和服种类繁多，男式和服款式简单；女式和服款式多样、图案高雅、色彩缤纷艳丽，有许多附属品和穿着规矩，根据不同场合穿着不同的款式，梳理不同的发型。

072

1991年熊本市市长田尻靖干赠和服套装

衣长152cm，胸围104cm；袖长32cm，宽48cm；腰带长138.5cm

High-end Kimono

Gift of Tajiri Yasumoto, the Mayor of Kumamoto, Japan, 1991

Length 152cm, chest 104cm; length of sleeve 32cm, width 48cm; length of belt 138.5cm

073

1992年日本加古川市议会议长联盟赠设色松树泥金折扇

通高22.6cm，通宽37.7cm

Folding Fan Painted with Pines (gold paper)

Gift of the Alliance of Speakers of Kakogawa Council, Japan, 1992

Overall height 22.6cm, overall width 37.7cm

团扇系中国的发明，而后传入日本；折扇出现于8世纪的奈良时期，是古代贵族阶层的手持物，后又传进中国。这在中日文化交流史上可谓趣事。当时，每逢夏季，宫廷贵族要赐予侍臣折扇，宫女受其影响，也常常带把折扇作为装饰品。人们的喜爱和日常生活的需要，促进了扇子的发展，出现了在扇面上作画、书写诗赋格言等。吉庆时，人们把折扇作为礼品赠送，象征着前途光明，人生之路愈走愈宽广。扇子作为道具，在舞台上被经常使用，表演者用扇子的张合、举动来表示剧中角色的心情。

074

1993年熊本市慈惠医院访华团赠持镜仕女人形

高37cm，底长19cm、宽14cm

Statue of a Geisha Girl Holding a Mirror

Gift of the Visiting Group of the Jikei Hospital in Kumamoto, Japan, 1993

Height 37cm, length of base 19cm, width of base 14cm

075

1994年日本小松市议会访华团赠五彩云鹤纹瓷盘

高6cm，直径31.5cm

Porcelain Plate with Polychrome Design of Cranes and Clouds

Gift of the Visiting Group of Council of Komatsu, Japan, 1994

Height 6cm, diameter 31.5cm

076

1994年日本创造美好人生访问团赠织锦风景画

通高48.1cm，通宽84.5cm；画心高37cm，宽68cm

Framed Tapestry of Landscape

Gift of the Visiting Group of Creating a Wonderful Life, Japan, 1994

Overall height 48.1cm, overall width 84.5cm; height of picture 37cm, width of picture 68cm

077

1996年熊本市市长三角保之赠熊本消防团纪念服

长89cm

Coat as a Souvenir of Kumamoto's Fire Department

Gift of the Mayor of Kumamoto, Japan, 1996

Length 89cm

078（上）

1978年泰国总理江萨赠镀金方盒

高6.4cm，长22.4cm，宽12.5cm

Gilded Box

Gift of Kriangsak Chomanan, the Prime Minister of Thailand, 1978

Height 6.4cm, length 22.4cm, width 12.5cm

079（下）

1978年泰国体育促进机构代表团赠红木方盒

高3.3cm，长18.9cm，宽10.3cm

Rosewood Box

Gift of the Delegation of Sports Promotion Organization of Thailand, 1978

Height 3.3cm, length 18.9cm, width 10.3cm

080

1978年泰国友谊旅行社访华团赠牛角孔雀雕塑

通高40cm

Ox Horn Sculpture of Peacock

Gift of the Delegation of Friendship Travel Agency from Thailand, 1978

Overall height 40cm

081

1978年泰国友谊旅行社九月团赠牛角龙船

高21.2cm，长71.2cm

Ox Horn Dragon Boat

Gift of the September Touring Group of Friendship Travel Agency from Thailand, 1978

Height 21.2cm, length 71.2cm

082

1979年泰国泰中友协代表团赠舞蹈玩具人

通高31.8cm

Toy Dancers

Gift of the Delegation of Thailand-China Friendship Association from Thailand, 1979

Overall height 31.8cm

083

1979年泰国艺术家代表团赠剪纸画挂屏

高16.5cm，长16.5cm

Paper-cut Hanging Panel

Gift of the Delegation of Artist from Thailand, 1979

Height 16.5cm, length 16.5cm

084

1979年泰国友谊旅行社五月团赠木象玩具

通高16cm

Toy of a Wood Elephant

Gift of the May Touring Group of Friendship Travel Agency from Thailand, 1979

Overall height 16cm

泰国是亚洲产象最多的国家，素有“大象之邦”的美称，用它来比喻国家繁荣昌盛、强大无比。在古代，大象曾被用于战争。泰国每年11月都在素辇举行盛大的象节，指挥官全身披挂古代的战服，威风凛凛地骑在象背上指挥士兵们作战，以纪念古代泰国人民为争取独立而进行的战斗。

085

1984年泰国访问团赠鎏金象战漆盘

直径25.2cm

Lacquer Plate with Gilded Design of Elephant War

Gift of the Delegation from Thailand, 1984

Diameter 25.2cm

086

1984年泰国农业新闻代表团赠鎏金紧那罗漆盘

直径35.2cm

Lacquer Plate with Gilded Design of Kinnara

Gift of the Delegation of Agriculture News from Thailand, 1984

Diameter 35.2cm

087

1983年泰国国会主席观光团赠泰中友谊纪念牌

高19.3cm，宽28.3cm

Memorial Plaque for Friendship between Thailand and China

Gift of the Touring Group of the President of the Parliament of Thailand, 1983

Height 19.3cm, width 28.3cm

088

1992年泰国孔敬市市长赠民族乐器

高101.5cm，宽17cm

National Musical Instrument

Gift of the Mayer of Khon Kaen City, Thailand, 1992

Height 101.5cm, width 17cm

089

2000年泰国内政部副次长赠手绘五彩素馨花纹盖罐

通高22.5cm，口径16.6cm

Covered Jar with Hand-drawn Polychrome Design of Jasminum Grandiflorum

Gift of the Vice Minister of the Ministry of the Interior of Thailand, 2000

Overall height 22.5cm, diameter of mouth 16.6cm

素馨花是泰国的国花，在瓷器上把素馨花画得如此精细传神实在是难能可贵。要在瓷器这种光滑、立体的器物上更为生动地表现，只有当画家纯熟、高超的技艺达到炉火纯青的境地时，艺术瓷——这一新的艺术表现形式便应运而生。

090

2000年泰国下议院秘书长赠手绘花边旧国会大厦瓷盘

高2.5cm，直径28cm

Porcelain Plate with Hand-drawn Design of the Ananda Samakhom Throne Hall and Floral Border

Gift of the Secretary-general of the House of Commons of Thailand, 2000

Height 2.5cm, diameter 28cm

旧国会大厦，是一座意大利文艺复兴式建筑，原是泰国五世王的王宫和议政院。七世王时，实行民主政治制度，改为国会。现在是王室博物馆。室内装饰金碧辉煌，有泰国历史演进的壁画。

091

1983年新加坡佳音合唱团赠鱼尾狮木雕

高25.5cm

Wooden Sculpture of the Merlion

Gift of the Good News Choral Society of Singapore, 1983

Height 25.5cm

新加坡著名的鱼尾狮像就坐落于新加坡河畔，是新加坡的标志和象征。该塑像高8米、重40吨，狮子口中喷出一股清水，是由雕刻家林南先生和他的两个孩子于1972年共同雕塑的。坐立在水波上的鱼尾狮，其设计概念是将事实和传说合二为一：狮头代表传说中的“狮城”新加坡；鱼尾象征古城“淡马锡”，代表新加坡是由一个小渔村发展起来的。据古书记载，古时新加坡叫作淡马锡，在爪哇语中为海城之意。14世纪时，传说有一个印尼的王子发现了这座小岛，他在这里看见一头神奇的野兽，后来得知是头狮子。就此，王子就将这座小岛命名为“Singapura”——在梵文里的意思是狮子（Singa）城（pura）。鱼尾狮座的铜匾上刻着：“鱼尾狮是新加坡迎宾好客的象征”。想必赠送者的意思是让我们团结起来，不分种族、语言和宗教信仰，怀抱新的精神，共同祝愿民主、和平、进步。

092

1991年新加坡总统黄金辉赠刻划松竹梅纹玻璃盘

口径34.7cm，底径14cm

Glass Plate with Incised Design of Pines, Bamboos and Plum Blossoms

Gift of Wee Kim Wee, the President of Singapore, 1991

Diameter of mouth 34.7cm, diameter of base 14cm

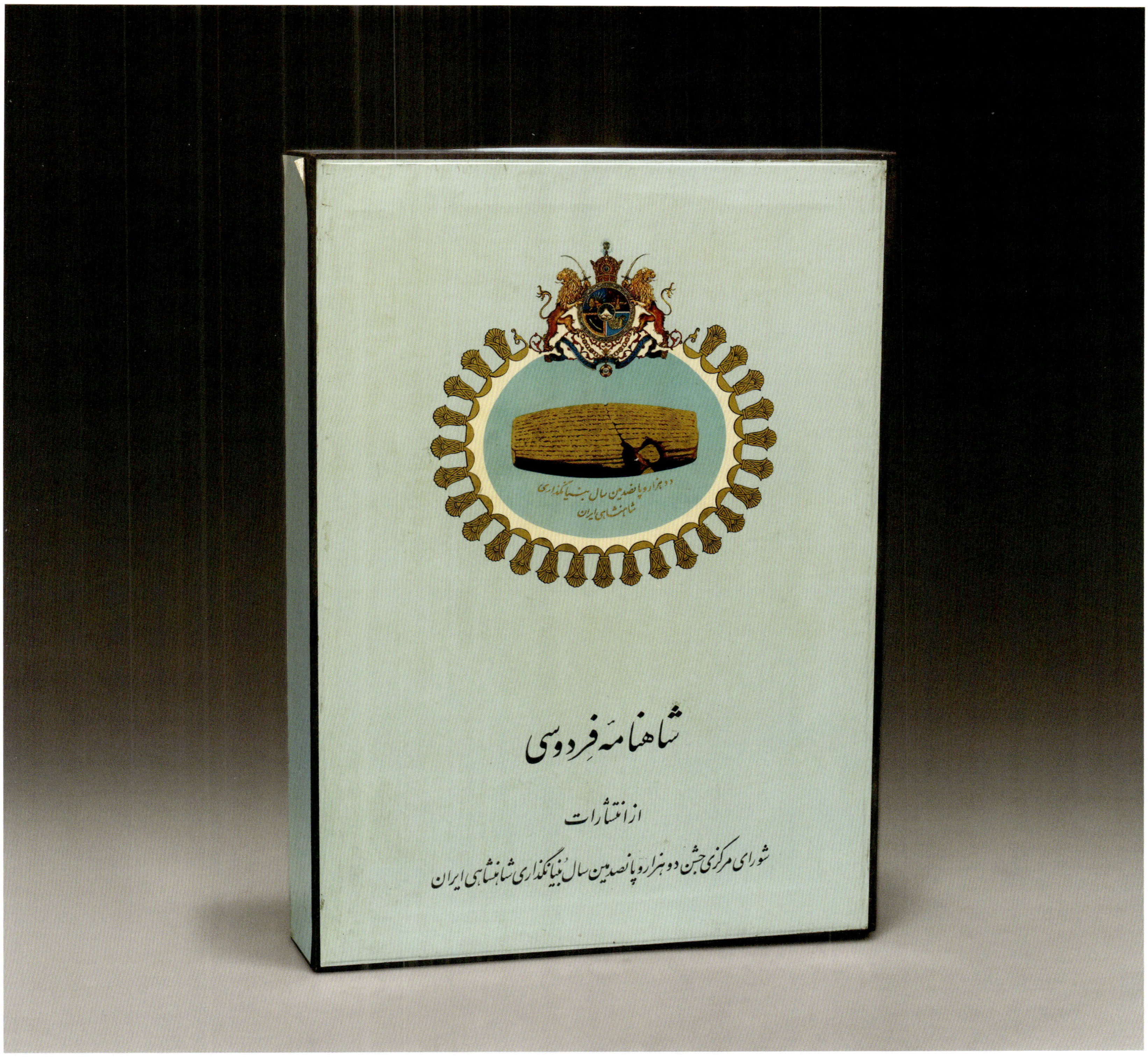

093

1976年伊朗公主赠精装金边《古兰经》

长39cm，宽28.5cm

The *Koran*, with Hard Cover and Gilded Edges

Gift of Iranian Princess, 1976

Length 39cm, width 28.5cm

094（上）

1982年印度驻华大使赠嵌玛瑙珠银烟盒

长11.4cm，宽7.6cm

Silver Cigarette Box Inlaid with Agate

Gift of India's Ambassador to China, 1982

Length 11.4cm, width 7.6cm

095（下）

1992年印度尼西亚最高评议院赠院徽纪念牌

高8cm，宽10cm，厚1cm

Memorial Plaque with Design of the Badge of the Supreme Advisory Council of the Republic of Indonesia

Gift of the Supreme Advisory Council of the Republic of Indonesia, 1992

Height 8cm, width 10cm, thickness 1cm

096

1992年印度尼西亚事业集团中央代表团赠纪念牌

高22.6cm，底座宽17.7cm

Memorial Plaque

Gift of Dewan Pimpinan Pusat Golongan Karya, Indonesia, 1992

Height 22.6cm, width of base 17.7cm

097

1974年越南领事赠独柱寺竹雕画

高39.6cm，宽28cm

Bamboo Carving of the One Pillar Pagoda

Gift of the Consul of Vietnam, 1974

Height 39.6cm, width 28cm

098（上）

1974年越南教育代表团赠越南漆画帆船

高34.9cm，宽50.1cm

Lacquer Painting of a Sailboat

Gift of the Educational Delegation from Vietnam, 1974

Height 34.9cm, width 50.1cm

099（下）

1974年越南教育代表团赠漆画战河

高30cm，宽45cm

Lacquer Painting of Battle by the River

Gift of the Educational Delegation from Vietnam, 1974

Height 30cm, width 45cm

100（上）

1974年越南教育代表团赠贝雕独柱寺风景画

高35cm，宽50cm

Shell Carving of the One Pillar Pagoda

Gift of the Educational Delegation from Vietnam, 1974

Height 35cm, width 50cm

101（下）

1974年越南教育代表团赠漆画独柱寺之秋

高35cm，宽50.2cm

Lacquer Painting of the Autumn of One Pillar Pagoda

Gift of the Educational Delegation from Vietnam, 1974

Height 35cm, width 50.2cm

102

1975年越南教育代表团赠铝制花瓶

高24cm，口径8.7cm

Aluminium Vase

Gift of the Educational Delegation from Vietnam, 1975

Height 24cm, diameter of mouth 8.7cm

103

1975年越南教育代表团赠独柱寺铜花瓶

高26cm，口径8cm

Bronze Vase with Design of the One Pillar Pagoda

Gift of the Educational Delegation from Vietnam, 1975

Height 26cm, diameter of mouth 8cm

104（上）

1975年越南教育部赠漆画独柱寺风光

高40cm，宽59.9cm

Lacquer Painting of the One Pillar Pagoda

Gift of the Ministry of Education of Vietnam, 1975

Height 40cm, width 59.9cm

105（下）

越南教育部赠解放南方铝片雕像

左（射击）：高12.6cm，宽11.5cm；右（冲锋）：高12.6cm，宽11.4cm

Aluminium Carvings of Liberation of the South of Vietnam

Gift of the Ministry of Education of Vietnam

Left (shooting): height 12.6cm, width 11.5cm; right (charging): height 12.6cm, width 11.4cm

106

1975年越南代表团赠漆画

高39.8cm，宽55cm

Lacquer Painting

Gift of the Delegation of Vietnam, 1975

Height 39.8cm, width 55cm

107

1978年越南代表团赠越南牛角龙船

长75.5cm

Ox Horn Dragon Boat

Gift of the Delegation of Vietnam, 1978

Length 75.5cm

108

1992年越南政府赠独柱寺木板漆画

高69.5cm，宽40cm

Lacquer Painting of the One Pillar Pagoda

Gift of the Vietnam Government, 1992

Height 69.5cm, width 40cm

109（上）

1992年越南政府赠银酒具

盘：高1.2cm，直径25.2cm；杯：高9.8cm，口径5cm；壶：高17.5cm，腹径9.3cm，通宽14.5cm

Silver Wine Set

Gift of the Vietnam Government, 1992

Plate: height 1.2cm, diameter 25.2cm; cup: height 9.8cm, diameter of mouth 5cm; teapot: height 17.5cm, diameter of belly 9.3cm, overall width 14.5cm

110（下）

越南独柱寺漆画盘

长25.2cm，宽15cm

Lacquer Plate with Design of the One Pillar Pagoda

Gift of Vietnam

Length 25.2cm, width 15cm

111（上）

1992年越南政府赠木漆画化妆盒

高6cm，长20.2cm，宽12.2cm

Makeup-box Decorated with Lacquer Painting

Gift of the Vietnam Government, 1992

Height 6cm, length 20.2cm, width 12.2cm

112（下）

越南独柱寺漆画茶叶漆盒

高8.8cm，口径7cm

Lacquer Tea Box with Design of the One Pillar Pagoda

Gift of Vietnam

Height 8.8cm, diameter of mouth 7cm

113（上）

越南铝制烟具

高10.5cm，长29cm，宽10cm

Aluminum Smoking Set

Gift of Vietnam

Height 10.5cm, length 29cm, width 10cm

114（下）

越南赠牛角人物雕像“冲锋”

高7cm，宽13.9cm

Ox Horn Carving of Charging

Gift of Vietnam

Height 7cm, width 13.9cm

第二单元　非洲礼品揽胜

非洲，是“阿非利加洲”的简称，位于东半球的西南部，面积约3020万平方千米，约占世界陆地总面积的20.2%。人口约10亿，约占世界人口总数的15%，仅次于亚洲，居世界第二位。

截止至2011年7月31日，已经与中国建立外交关系的非洲国家有50个。

非洲是古人类和文明的发祥地之一，勤劳智慧的非洲人民创造了辉煌灿烂的古代文明，在建筑、雕刻和绘画艺术等方面取得了巨大成就，留下了丰富的文化遗产。非洲礼品具有浓郁的地域文化特色，展示出迷人的风采。其中，雕刻在世界艺术之林中占有十分重要的地位。它以象征性的造型艺术语言表达着非洲各部落的民俗风情、宗教信仰和美学观念，具有极其感人的，淳朴、粗犷、强烈的形象性，同时也展示出非洲人特有的大胆和创造精神。来自文明古国埃及的两只精美的铜盘，刻画着闻名世界的古埃及文明的象征——金字塔，记载着辉煌的历史和美丽的神话。而那些技艺精湛的铜塑制品，均展示出非洲人特有的创造力。铜器上的每一件雕刻都有其特定的寓意，蕴含着深层的文化。

Chapter 2　African Gifts

Africa, short for "African continent", lies in the southwest of the eastern hemisphere. It covers an area of around 30.2 million square kilometers, accounting for nearly 20.2% of the world's total land area. Its population is around one billion and takes up nearly 15% of the whole world population, ranking second in the world, next only to Asia.

Till July 31st, 2011, 50 African countries had established diplomatic relations with China.

Africa is one of the birthplaces of primitive human beings and civilization. Having created glorious and splendid ancient civilization, industrious and ingenious African people make tremendous achievement in architecture, sculpture, painting and other aspects, and leave behind abundant cultural heritage. With rich regional cultural characteristics, African gifts show fascinating elegance. In the forest of world arts, sculpture takes a very important position. With symbolic molding art language, it expresses folk customs, religious faith and aesthetic concepts of African tribes. It not merely features impressive simple, bold and strong image, but also demonstrates African people's typical daring and creation spirit. The carving of Pyramid, the symbol of the world renowned ancient Egypt civilization, on the two exquisite brass plates from the ancient civilized country — Egypt, records the glorious history and beautiful myth. The exquisite bronze products demonstrate the extraordinary creativity of African people. Every carving on the bronze ware has its special implications and reflects profound culture.

115（上）

1982年埃及通用公司赠鎏金神话故事铜工艺盘

直径24.7cm

Bronze Plate with Gilded Design of Egyptian Mythology

Gift of General Company of Egypt, 1982

Diameter 24.7 cm

116（下）

1982年埃及通用公司赠鎏金法老车驾图铜工艺盘

直径30cm

Bronze Plate with Gilded Design of Pharaoh Driving Carriage

Gift of General Company of Egypt, 1982

Diameter 30 cm

古埃及在建筑、雕刻和绘画等艺术方面取得了巨大成就。铜盘刻画的古埃及文明的象征——金字塔，是公元前27世纪前后古埃及人的杰作，是人类建筑史上的奇迹。金字塔前，一男子驾着马车张弓射箭，他头上的冠帽象征其法老身份。铜盘上记载着辉煌的历史和美丽的神话，反映了埃及历史上那个时代经济、政治和社会大变革。

117

1974年刚果代表团赠乌木人头雕像

高26cm，宽21.5cm

Ebony Head

Gift of the Delegation from Congo, 1974

Height 26cm, width 21.5cm

118

1977年喀麦隆总统阿希乔赠铜铸图腾面具挂饰

高57cm，宽40cm

Bronze Totem Mask

Gift of Ahmadou Ahidjo, the President of Cameroon, 1977

Height 57cm, width 40cm

非洲雕刻是一种象征艺术，它以独特的造型艺术语言表现出非洲原始部落的社会风俗、宗教信仰和美学观念，每一个雕刻图案都有其特定的寓意，蕴含着深层的文化。

喀麦隆有着悠久的历史和文化，公元5世纪起，喀麦隆就已先后形成一些部落王国和部落联盟国家。14世纪晚期在喀麦隆东部建立的巴蒙王国，形成了与其他部族完全不同的文化形态，他们在铜雕、陶器、木雕、纺织等方面具有高度的艺术水平。巴蒙王国的铜雕艺术有着辉煌的历史，曾有过先进的黄铜铸造中心。黄铜被视为高贵之物，只有统治者才有权享用黄铜制品。

巴蒙王国的这副面具与当地人的意识形态有密不可分的联系。当地人认为，人死后的灵魂脱离躯体、自由游荡，会使生者烦恼，扰乱社会秩序。面具有捕获和控制灵魂的作用，因而他们制作千姿百态的面具，以纪念死者、保护生者。非洲当地各族都有自己的图腾，他们相信，对图腾的真诚膜拜能使本族人与图腾产生交感，从而得到图腾的生机、活力与魔力，把图腾铸在面具上，可以避邪纳祥。这副面具中的人像是一副微笑的表情，双睛圆鼓，瞳孔突出，嘴巴张开，牙齿外露，头饰上雕有双头蛇、蜥蜴、青蛙、羚羊等动物形象，最下部是象征着胡须的装饰。通过象征符号语言表现，是巴蒙王室艺术的重要特征，以此强调统治者拥有至高无上的权力。面具中的嘴巴作说话状，传达的是一种神圣的权力。蜥蜴和青蛙具有很强的繁殖力，因此被用来象征王朝的丰产与增长。而双头蛇形象则与王朝历史和军事力量有关。巴蒙王国的第十一代君主穆博奥姆布欧（1820～1840年在位）是一位英明果断、骁勇善战的统治者。传说他身高2.6米，手杖长2米，力大无穷，能空手与河马博斗；吼声如雷，一声怒吼可传至数里以外，令敌人闻风丧胆。他作战勇猛，身先士卒，所到之处敌人不战而降。穆博奥姆布欧将巴蒙王国的疆域扩张了20倍，征服了48个酋长部落，为王朝立下赫赫功劳。他亲自设计战旗，即如今巴蒙王国的国徽“双头蛇八角蛛”。在对外征战中，因为他在战场上能够同时前后作战，因而被比作双头蟒蛇。面具在反映祖先崇拜的传统信仰时，更传递了王室权威思想：统治者具有保卫、管理、促进王国繁荣的神圣权力。面具顶部神武的勇士双手握着两条蛇，应该就是那位受人景仰的穆博奥姆布欧国王。

119

1977年喀麦隆总统阿希乔赠铜钟铃

通高45cm，底径15cm

Bronze Bell

Gift of Ahmadou Ahidjo, the President of Cameroon, 1977

Overall height 45cm, diameter of base 15cm

铜钟铃是另一件引人注目的精致工艺品：一条双头蛇盘绕站立，铃上装饰有蜘蛛、青蛙、鹰鸟等图案。巴蒙人崇拜蛇和蜘蛛。他们认为蛇是威严和力量的化身，它的两个头象征国王当年兵分两路打击敌人，并取得决定性胜利。铃铛内悬挂一只八角形的蜘蛛。巴蒙人认为，蜘蛛能预卜未来，是凡人和造物主之间的信使，是智慧的源泉。而钟铃一经摇动，能发出两种不同的声音，武士们能凭直觉辨别出是进军的号角还是撤退的命令。据说从穆博奥姆布欧国王在位的时代起，它一直是巴蒙王国王室权威与尊严的最重要的象征物。在巴蒙王国的重要建筑上、出版的书籍上，乃至一些工艺品上，显著位置都标有这件圣物的图案。

120

1977年喀麦隆总统阿希乔赠铜铸骑士

高54cm

Bronze Statue of a Horsing Man

Gift of Ahmadou Ahidjo, the President of Cameroon, 1977

Height 54cm

铜铸就的骑士，所反映的应是巴蒙王国的第十一代君主穆博奥姆布欧征战的雄姿。他骑在前腿腾空的战马上，头戴战盔，身穿铠甲，手持战刀，准备与敌人厮杀。这件铜铸工艺品，人物造型夸张，战马富有生气。而与马后腿相连的圈足，既解决了刻画人物的需要，又使作品获得稳定。

121

1977年喀麦隆总统阿希乔赠蛇皮纹串珠铁手杖

长96.5cm，直径1.5cm

Iron Cane Decorated with Beaded Snake Skin

Gift of Ahmadou Ahidjo, the President of Cameroon, 1977

Length 96.5cm, diameter 1.5cm

蛇皮纹串珠装饰的铁手杖仿佛让人领略了巴蒙国王穆博奥姆布欧手持两米长的手杖，身先士卒、所向披靡、奋勇杀敌的英雄气概。

122

1999年科特迪瓦矿业石油资源部部长赠铜制少女头像

通高61.8cm，通宽45.9cm，厚12.5cm

Bronze Head of a Girl

Gift of the Minister of Ministry of Mine, Petroleum and Resource of Coate D'lvorie, 1999

Overall height 61.8cm, overall width 45.9cm, thickness 12.5cm

123

1990年摩洛哥外交国务秘书赠刻划花卉纹镀银托盘

高37.5cm，宽54.7cm

Slivering Tray with Incised Decoration of Flowers

Gift of the Secretary of Ministry of Foreign and National Affairs, Morocco, 1990

Height 37.5cm, width 54.7cm

124

1981年苏丹总理赠蓝釉贴金瓷茶具

杯高7cm；碟径15cm；茶叶壶高11.5cm；茶壶高17.5cm；奶罐高9.5cm

Porcelain Tea Set with Blue Glaze and Gold Leaves

Gift of the Premier of Sudan, 1981

Height of cup 7cm; diameter of tray 15cm; height of tea container 11.5cm; height of teapot 17.5cm; height of milk container 9.5cm

125

1980年突尼斯友好人士费尔穆赠背壶少女瓷板画

高2.1cm，宽1.6cm

Porcelain Plate Painted with a Girl Holding a Vessel on Back

Gift of Fireman, a Friendly Personality of Tunisia, 1980

Height 2.1cm, width 1.6cm

第三单元　美洲礼品揽胜

美洲，是“亚美利加洲”的简称，位于西半球。美洲以巴拿马运河为界，分为北美洲和南美洲，面积约4219.8万平方千米，约占世界陆地总面积的28%。人口约7.5亿。

截止至2011年7月31日，有23个美洲国家与我国建立了外交关系。

作为“新大陆”，美洲既有高度发达的现代科技，也有淳朴的印第安风情，并且汇聚了丰富多彩的移民文化。美洲国家的礼品反映了美洲古老的文明，也秉承了欧洲艺术的传统，更突出了浓郁的历史文化氛围。美国的铜铃、铜钥匙蕴含着丰富的文化内涵；和平之鸟瓷盘，表达了和平的祈愿；电版画反映了印第安西海岸独特的设计艺术；羊毛斗篷、方巾等传统服饰颇具民族特色，让中国人民更好地了解了当地的服饰文化。

Chapter 3 American Gifts

America, short for "American continent", lies in the western hemisphere. Taking Panama Canal as the sector, America is divided into North America and South America. It covers an area of around 42.198 million square kilometers, accounting for nearly 28% of the world's total land area. Its population is around 750 million

Till July 31st, 2011, 23 American countries had established diplomatic relations with China.

As the "New World", America not only has highly developed modern technology, but also keeps Indian folk customs and integrates a variety of colorful immigrant cultures. Gifts from America not simply reflect the ancient American civilization, but also inherit the tradition of European art and highlight the dense historical and cultural atmosphere. American bronze bells and bronze keys entail rich cultural connotations; porcelain plate decorated with swans expresses prayer for peace; electric prints reflect the unique design art of the Indian west coast; wool cape, scarf and other traditional clothing feature ethnic characteristics, helping Chinese people better understand the local clothing culture.

126

1978年加拿大友人赠木天鹅

长6.6cm，厚1.8cm

Wood Carving of a Swan

Gift of Friends from Canada, 1978

Length 6.6cm, thickness 1.8cm

127

1983年加拿大艾伯塔省省长洛希德赠纪念币套装

高15.8cm，横10.8cm，厚2.5cm

A Series of Memorial Coins

Gift of Peter Lougheed, the Governor of Alberta, Canada, 1983

Hight 15.8cm, width 10.8cm, thickness 2.5cm

128

1976年美国前总统尼克松赠瓷熊猫

高16cm，长20cm

Porcelain Panda

Gift of Richard Milhous Nixon, the Former President of America, 1976

Height 16cm, length 20cm

熊猫是中国的国宝，随着中美关系的解冻，中国政府于1972年4月赠送给美国一对大熊猫“玲玲”和“兴兴”，当时轰动美国，每年平均有300多万美国人到华盛顿国家动物园观看。熊猫温和可爱，成为和平使者。

该瓷熊猫制作于1974年。

129

1976年美国前总统尼克松赠和平之鸟镀金骨瓷盘

高2cm，直32.8cm

Porcelain Plate Decorated with Swans and Gilded Border

Gift of Richard Milhous Nixon, the Former President of America, 1976

Height 2cm, diameter 32.8cm

和平之鸟瓷盘和瓷熊猫是由美国著名的新泽西州波姆陶瓷艺术中心烧制的。1976年，美国前总统尼克松先生访问桂林，将这两件珍贵的工艺品赠送给桂林人民，表达了美国人民对桂林人民的情谊。

1972年2月，美国总统尼克松历史性地访问中国，赠送给毛泽东主席的国礼——瓷塑“和平之鸟”，正是由该中心所创烧的。当时，还限量版烧制了“和平之鸟”镀金骨瓷盘。作品将天鹅繁衍、哺育和爱抚后代的神形姿态塑造得惟妙惟肖，呈现出安谧、和平的优美意境。

天鹅是美国人民最喜爱的吉祥动物之一，传说它能够给人类带来幸福和好运。瓷盘中绘着两只大天鹅和几只小天鹅在荷花中嬉戏，象征着一个幸福愉快的家庭。它是和平、友善的使者，寄托了尼克松对中美友好关系的展望。

130

1983年美国西雅图—重庆友城协会赠波音747飞机模型

高35cm，宽30cm

Boeing 747 Model

Gift of Seattle-Chongqing Friendship Association of America, 1983

Height 35cm, width 30cm

131

1985年美国驻广州总领事赠银果盘

高8cm，口径24.8cm

Silver Fruit Tray

Gift of the American Consul General of Guangzhou, 1985

Height 8cm, diameter of mouth 24.8cm

132

1985年美国奥兰多市长比尔·弗雷德里克赠奥兰多水晶城徽印

高12.6cm，宽21.8cm

Crystal Engraved with Orlando's City Badge

Gift of Bill Frederick, the Mayor of Orlando, America, 1985

Height 12.6cm, width 21.8cm

在两市缔结友好城市的仪式上，奥兰多市市长比尔·弗雷德里克亲手把刻有奥兰多市徽的金钥匙和水晶城徽郑重送给桂林市政府和人民，它们是奥兰多市的象征，作为"忠诚、可靠、信赖"的信物。之后，历届奥兰多市长都将这珍贵的礼物馈赠给桂林人民。

133（上）

1985年奥兰多市长赠镀金钥匙

高6.7cm，长20cm

Gilded Key of Orlando

Gift of the Mayor of Orlando, America, 1985

Height 6.7cm, width 20cm

134（下）

1986年美国大企业090927团赠镀金熊摆件

通高15.5cm

Gilded Bear

Gift of the No. 090927 Delegation of Large Enterprise of America, 1986

Overall height 15.5cm

135

1990年美国奥兰多市长比尔·弗雷德里克赠镀铜铝版风景画

高41.8cm，宽48.4cm

Aluminum Plate with Copper Plating Landscape

Gift of Bill Frederick, the Mayor of Orlando, America, 1990

Height 41.8cm, width 48.4cm

136（上）

1992年美国奥兰多市长比尔·弗雷德里克赠桂林袁凤兰市长刻花镀银盘

高3.8cm，宽30.7cm

Silvering Plate with Incised Design of Flowers

Gift of Bill Frederick, the Mayor of Orlando, America, to Yuan Fenglan, the Mayor of Guilin, 1992

Height 3.8cm, width 30.7cm

137（下）

1992年美国奥兰多市长比尔·弗雷德里克赠刻字镀银盘

高2.5cm，宽39.6cm

Silvering Plate with Incised Characters

Gift of Bill Frederick, the Mayor of Orlando, America, 1992

Height 2.5cm, width 39.6cm

138（上）

1992年美国奥兰多市长赠金钥匙

高11cm，宽20.4cm

Golden Key of Orlando

Gift of the Mayor of Orlando, America, 1992

Height 11cm, width 20.4cm

139（下）

美国奥兰多市长格兰达·E. 胡德赠奥兰多市金钥匙

高8.5cm，宽18.6cm，厚3cm

Golden Key of Orlando

Gift of Glenda E. Hood, the Mayor of Orlando, America

Height 8.5cm, width18.6cm, thickness 3cm

140

1992年美国德克萨斯州加兰市刘氏投资公司总裁赠陶工艺盘

高2.5cm，直径20.9cm

Pottery Plate

Gift of the President of Lau's Investment Company, Garland, Texas, America, 1992

Height 2.5cm, diameter 20.9cm

141

1979年智利体育代表团赠工艺铜鸟

高40cm，厚3.4cm

Bronze Bird

Gift of the Sport Delegation of Chile, 1979

Height 40cm, thickness 3.4cm

142

1978年墨西哥友人赠工艺草帽

直径8.4cm

Craft Straw Hat

Gift of Mexican Friends, 1978

Diameter 8.4cm

第四单元　大洋洲礼品揽胜

大洋洲，原意为“大洋中的陆地”，位于太平洋西南部和赤道南北的广大海域中。陆地连同岛屿总面积约897万平方千米，约占世界陆地总面积的6%，是世界上最小的洲。居民由土著居民和外来居民共同构成。

截止至2011年7月31日，与我国建立外交关系的大洋洲国家有10个。

大洋洲自然资源丰富，大洋洲国家的礼品突出表现了其物产和文化特色，反映出浓郁的民情风俗，使人领略到大洋洲迷人的风情。生动可爱的镀银树袋熊、袋鼠图巾，反映了澳大利亚独特的生态环境；新西兰风土人情地图画，反映了当地毛利人的重要文化习俗；萨摩亚的贝壳项链是土著人喜爱的装饰品，体现了土著人特有的馈赠礼俗；还有积淀了丰富文化传统的土著居民原始木雕艺术品，凸显了大洋洲独一无二的特性。

Chapter 4 Oceanian Gifts

Oceania, originally meaning "land of the ocean", lies in the vast water area between the southwest Pacific and the north and south of the equator. The total land and island area is around 8.97 million square kilometers, accounting for nearly 6% of the world's total land area. It is the smallest continent in the world. Its inhabitants mainly consist of indigenous people and foreign residents.

Till July 31st, 2011, 10 Oceanian countries had established diplomatic relations with China.

Oceania boasts abundant natural resources. Gifts from Oceanian countries highlight Oceanian product and cultural characteristics. They reflect strong flavor of ethnic culture and folk customs, making people appreciate the glamour of Oceania. Vivid and lovely silvered koala bear and towels with kangaroo patterns show the unique ecological environment of Australia; New Zealand custom map painting gives an account of the important local cultural practices of Maori people; as indigenous people's favorite ornament, Samoa shell necklace represents indigenous people's unique gift presenting etiquette; with rich cultural heritage, indigenous people's original wood carving artwork highlights the unique characteristics of Oceania.

143

1977年澳大利亚友人赠悉尼歌剧院模型

高4.1cm，长6.4cm，宽4.7cm

Sydney Opera House Model

Gift of Australian Friends, 1977

Height 4.1cm, length 6.4cm, width 4.7cm

悉尼歌剧院位于澳大利亚悉尼，是20世纪最具特色的建筑之一，也是世界著名的表演艺术中心，已成为悉尼市的标志性建筑。歌剧院座落于悉尼市区北部，贝壳形屋顶下方是结合剧院和厅室的综合建筑。从20世纪50年代开始构思兴建，1956年起公开征求世界各地的设计作品，共有32个国家的233件作品参选，结果丹麦建筑师约恩·乌赞的设计“雀屏”中选。但后来因施工困难及经费不断追加等问题，乌赞与当地政府失和，于1966年愤而离去，从此未再踏上澳大利亚土地。歌剧院后来由一群澳大利亚建筑师接手完成。悉尼歌剧院共耗时16年，斥资1200万澳币，于1973年10月20日正式竣工开幕。2007年被联合国教科文组织评为世界文化遗产。

144

1978年澳大利亚友人赠浮雕烟碟

长13cm，宽11cm

Ashtray with Relief Decoration

Gift of Australian Friends, 1978

Length 13cm, width 11cm

145

1991年澳大利亚地方政府代表团赠米查姆市城徽纪念牌

高21cm，宽9.6cm，厚1.8cm

Souvenir Plate of Mitcham's City Emblem

Gift of the Members of the Australian Local Government Delegation, 1991

Height 21cm, width 9.6cm, thickness 1.8cm

146

1993年澳大利亚外交部长赠镀银树袋熊

高5.8cm，腹径8.4cm

Silvering Koala Bear

Gift of the Minister of Foreign Affairs of Australia, 1993

Height 5.8cm, diameter of belly 8.4cm

树袋熊又叫考拉、无尾熊，英语名koala bear，是澳大利亚原住民的方言，意指“不喝水”。树袋熊身体长70~80厘米，成年体重8~15千克，无尾，长相酷似小熊，性情温顺，体态憨厚。无尾熊是澳大利亚的国宝，面值200澳元的金币上铸着它们可爱的形象，每年10月20日为澳大利亚全国无尾熊日。

147

1976年新西兰代表团赠风土人情地图画

高80cm，宽50cm

Painting of Local Customs and Lives

Gift of the Delegation from New Zealand, 1976

High 80cm, width 50cm

148

1981年黑斯廷斯市市长赠木船雕

长16cm，宽14cm

Wood Carving Boat

Gift of the Mayor of Hastings, New Zealand, 1981

Length 16cm, width 14cm

新西兰的土著居民是毛利人，毛利木雕是新西兰文化艺术的瑰宝，体现了毛利的文化特征。新西兰木雕各具特色，题材有花果、鸟兽等，装饰方法有浮雕、透雕、镶嵌等，再加上能工巧匠的装饰、文人墨士的渲染，赋予了各种灵性色彩。

这一件木头船雕，首尾高翘，底部浑圆，形制娇巧风趣。独步舟在新西兰历史上具有重要的意义。传说10世纪时，有一位名叫库佩的波利尼西亚人，因为追捕一条大章鱼而发现了这块美丽的土地。到了14世纪中叶，大批波利尼西亚人分乘七艘独木舟，远涉重洋抵达这里。他们从不同的地点登陆，并建立了个各自的居住点，由此形成了今日人们所知的七个主要部落。在我们所陈列的独木舟上雕刻有各式人物，这一般被认为是毛利人的祖先或者是杰出的部落首领，他们可以保佑新西兰人在海上平安航行。

149

1981年新西兰威廉姆斯赠嵌贝工艺盘

直径7.1cm

Plate Inlaid with Shells

Gift of Williams from New Zealand, 1981

Diameter 7.1cm

150

1983年新西兰黑斯廷斯市市长赠木雕几维鸟摆件

高15.8cm，宽13.3cm

Wood Carving of Kiwi

Gift of the Mayor of Hastings, New Zealand, 1983

Height 15.8cm, width 13.3cm

几维鸟是新西兰的国鸟，这是因为新西兰是目前世界上唯一有几维鸟生存的国家。几维鸟外形奇特，它是最不像鸟的鸟类，没有胸骨，没有尾巴，几乎没有翅膀，所以又被称为“无翅鸟”。在过去，毛利人常用几维鸟的羽毛编织衣服，今天，用几维鸟羽毛制作的几维席仍是新西兰最名贵的特产。

几维鸟被视为新西兰国家的象征，在新西兰几乎随处可以看见与几维鸟有关的东西，如国徽钱币、产品商标等。

151

1985年新西兰赠木雕人

高47.5cm，长9.7cm，宽9.3cm

Wood Carving of a Figure

Gift of New Zealand, 1985

Height 47.5cm, length 9.7cm, width 9.3cm

新西兰的木雕人是毛利人信仰和崇拜的祖先形象，毛利人经常使用新西兰特产的一种软玉雕刻这类人像并挂在自己胸前。其形状基本上以固定的模式出现：四方形的头与肩部同宽，大而圆的眼睛用贝壳做镶嵌，鼻子在两眼之间与额头相连，嘴巴非常大，长长的舌头从露在嘴角外面的牙齿中间伸出，双手交叉在胸前，各伸三指，脚弯曲。当地传说佩带这种“海蒂基”，便可以得到神灵的保佑。

152

1985年黑斯廷斯市市长赠花鸟木雕挂饰

高69cm，宽49cm

Hanging Decoration of Wood Carving Flowers and Birds

Gift of the Mayor of Hastings, New Zealand, 1985

Height 69cm, width 49cm

153

1987年黑斯廷斯市市长赠木雕挂饰

高48.2cm，宽10cm

Hanging Decoration of Wood Carving

Gift of the Mayor of Hastings, New Zealand, 1987

Height 48.2cm, width 10cm

154

1988年新西兰文化艺术部部长赠瓷盅

通高5.5cm，直径7.5cm

Porcelain Cup

Gift of the Minister of Culture and Art of New Zealand, 1988

Overall height 5.5cm, diameter 7.5cm

155

1988年新西兰黑斯廷斯市友好访华团赠彩绘瓷碗

高9cm，口径27.9cm，底径10cm

Porcelain Bowl Painted with Colorful Flowers

Gift of the Friendly Visiting Group of Hastings, New Zealand, 1988

Height 9cm, diameter of mouth 27.9cm, diameter of base 10cm

这只黄彩饰的瓷碗，色彩斑斓，胎质洁白，釉面呈黄色，自然而古朴，现为毛利人爱用和收藏的宠物。这种瓷碗在毛利人生活中，是一种具有特殊作用的“宝碗”，用来装果、麦和豆子。它在婚礼中使用，是一种象征繁殖的器物。黄色衬花于碗中，表示祝愿接受此碗者一年四季平安愉快，这只碗里面有三朵花蕾，意为“祝您即将平安地连升三级”。

156

1990年黑斯廷斯市市长杰莱米・德埃尔赠工艺木雕罐

高26cm，口径12cm，腰围68cm，底径8.3cm

Wood Jar

Gift of Jeremy de El, the Mayor of Hastings, New Zealand, 1990

Height 26cm, diameter of mouth 12cm, waistline 68cm, diameter of base 8.3cm

157（上）

1990年黑斯廷斯市市长杰莱米·德埃尔赠工笔重彩花鸟画挂饰

高19.9cm，宽15.2cm

Hanging Decorations with Flower-bird Fine Brushwork in Heavy Color

Gift of Jeremy de El, the Mayor of Hastings, New Zealand, 1990

Height 19.9cm, width 15.2cm

158（下）

1990年新西兰友好代表团赠黑斯廷斯市徽五彩瓷盘

高2.2cm，口径19.8cm，底径13.4cm

Porcelain Plate Painted in Overglaze Polychrome Design of Hastings's City Emblem

Gift of the Friendly Delegation of New Zealand, 1990

Height 2.2cm, diameter of mouth 19.8cm, diameter of base 13.4cm

159（上）

1991年新西兰黑斯廷斯市政府赠油画《蒂玛塔山雄姿》

高37cm，宽47.5cm

Oil Painting of the Te Mata Hills

Gift of the Hastings Government, New Zealand, 1991

Height 37cm, width 47.5cm

160（下）

1991年新西兰政府赠蓝釉葡萄纹大盘

高6.5cm，口径39.5cm，底径25.5cm

Blue-glazed Plate w th Design of Grapes

Gift of New Zealanc Government, 1991

Height 6.5cm, diame.er of mouth 39.5cm, diameter of base 25.5cm

161（上）

1992年新西兰黑斯廷斯市议会团赠木制水果及木盒

盒：高10cm，口径24.8cm；水果：高5.1cm，直径6.1～9.7cm

Wood Carving of Fruits and Box

Gift of the Hastings Parliament Group , New Zealand, 1992

Box: height 10cm, diameter of mouth 24.8cm; fruit: height 5.1cm, diameter 6.1~9.7cm

162（下）

1993年新西兰霍克赠油画《牧羊图》（1990年作）

通高83cm，通宽92cm；画心高52.5cm，宽61cm

Oil Painting of Herding (painted in 1990)

Gift of Hawker from New Zealand, 1993

Overall height 83cm, overall width 92cm; painting: height 52.5cm, width 61cm

163

1993年黑斯廷斯市商会访华团赠新西兰地图挂饰

高81cm，宽28cm

Hanging Tapestry with Design of New Zealand

Gift of Hastings Chamber of Commerce Delegation, New Zealand, 1993

Height 81cm, width 28cm

164

1994年黑斯廷斯地区议会代表团赠木碗

高5.2cm，口径20cm

Wood Bowl

Gift of the Hastings Local Parliament Delegation, New Zealand, 1994

Height 5.2cm, diameter of mouth 20cm

165（上）

1994年黑斯廷斯地区议会代表团赠木碗

高7cm，口径16cm

Wood Bowl

Gift of the Hastings Local Parliament Delegation, New Zealand, 1994

Height 7cm, diameter of mouth 16cm

166（下）

1994年黑斯廷斯地区议会代表团赠镂孔木盒

通高9.8cm，口径8.9cm，腹径10.7cm

Openwork Wooden Box

Gift of the Hastings Local Parliament Delegation, New Zealand, 1994

Overall height 9.8cm, diameter of mouth 8.9cm, diameter of belly 10.7cm

167

1999年黑斯廷斯市市长杰莱米·德埃尔赠彩绘果蔬漆盘

高1.8cm，直径15.5cm

Lacquer Plate Painted with Fruits and Vegetables

Gift of Jeremy de El, the Mayor of Hastings, New Zealand, 1999

Height 1.8cm, diameter 15.5cm

第五单元　欧洲礼品揽胜

欧洲，是“欧罗巴洲”的简称，位于东半球西北部，面积约1016万平方千米，约占世界陆地总面积的6.8%。人口约7.27亿，是人口最密集的一个洲。欧洲大陆地形以平原为主，其次是丘陵和山地。这里河网稠密，自然资源丰富，经济发达。

截止至2011年7月31日，有44个欧洲国家与中国建立了外交关系。

欧洲国家的礼品大多以欧洲传统艺术和文化理念为基础，展示出独特的风格和艺术造诣，又突出了浓郁的历史氛围，形成了欧洲艺术多姿多彩的面貌。晶莹剔透、熠熠生辉的玻璃北极熊，象征着友情的纯净和稳固；雕塑母狼源于一个美丽的传说；西德瓷酒壶更是形制优雅、釉色明丽；而那些质地沉重的铜塑制品，具有淳朴、粗犷和强烈的想象性，均体现了欧洲王室宫廷的豪华气派。

Chapter 5 European Gifts

Europe, short for "Europa Continent", lies in the northwest of the eastern hemisphere. It covers an area of around 10.16 million square kilometers, accounting for nearly 6.8% of the world's total land area. With the population of around 727 million, Europe is the most densely populated continent. As for the topographic features, European Continent is mainly based on plain, next to which are hills and mountains. With dense water network, Europe has abundant natural resources and developed economy.

Till July 31st, 2011, 44 European countries had established diplomatic relations with China.

Mainly based on European traditional arts and cultural concepts, gifts from European countries not only display unique styles and artistic attainments, but also highlight dense history atmosphere, presenting a colorful look of European art. Crystal clear, sparkling glass polar bear symbolizes pure and solid friendship; female sculpture originates from a beautiful legend; West Germany porcelain wine jug features elegant shape and bright glaze; heavy copper products, characterized by simplicity, ruggedness and wild imagination, show the magnificence of European royal palace.

168（上）

1975年奥地利中国研究会代表团赠合金小盘

直径15cm

Metal Plate

Gift of China Research Society, Austria, 1975

Diameter 15cm

169（下）

1978年奥地利中国研究会赠徽章纹小瓷盅

通高8cm，口径8.1cm

Armorial Porcelain Bowls

Gift of China Research Society, Austria, 1978

Overall height 8cm, diameter of mouth 8.1cm

170

1994年奥地利联邦议会代表团赠徽章纹镀银盘

高1cm，直径21.7cm

Silvering Armorial Plate

Gift of the Austrian Federal Parliament Delegation, 1994

Height 1cm, diameter 21.7cm

171

1978年保加利亚科技代表团赠彩绘木盒

通高6.2cm，口径7.1cm

Wood Box Decorated with Colored Drawings

Gift of the Science and Technology Delegation of Bulgaria, 1978

Overall height 6.2cm, diameter of mouth 7.1cm

172

1981年比利时国王和王后赠铜人雕像

通高7.7cm

Bronze Sculpture of a Man

Gift of the King and Queen of Belgium, 1981

Overall height 7.7cm

1981年比利时国王和王后赠送的铜人，一手持枪，一手握着被掐断的铁链，代表了比利时人民为争取独立和自由而英勇不屈的民族精神。

173

1981年比利时国王和王后赠玻璃四方瓶

高27cm，宽20.3 cm

Glass Bottle

Gift of the King and Queen of Belgium, 1981

Height 27cm, width 20.3cm

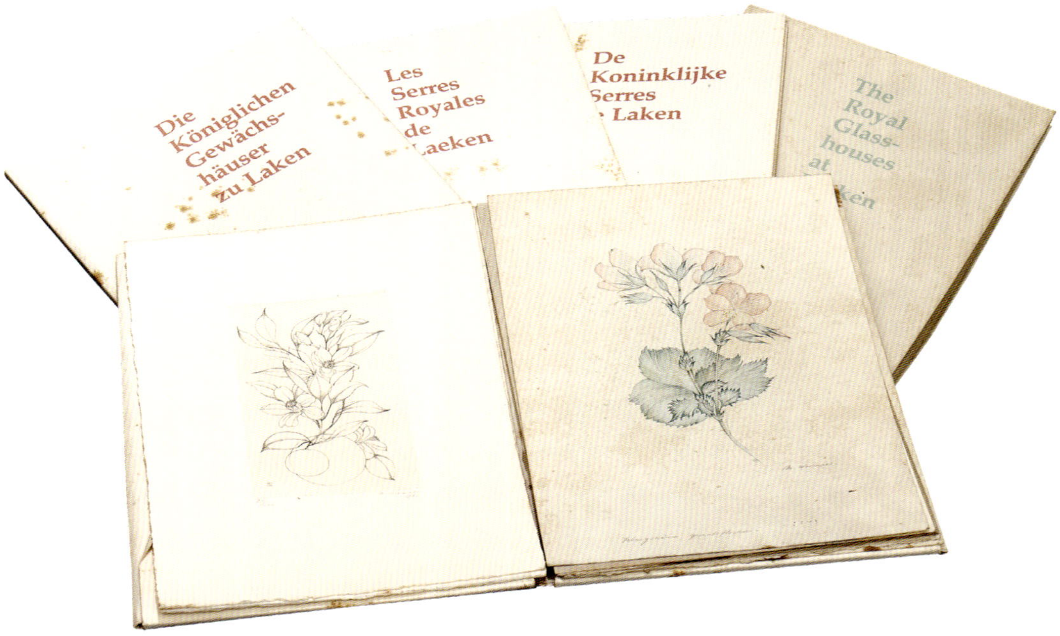

174（上）

1981年比利时国王赠手绘淡彩书画册

长36cm，宽24cm

Albums of Hand Drawn Paintings

Gift of the King of Belgium, 1981

Length 36cm, width 24cm

175（下）

1981年比利时国王和王后赠陶纪念章

长80cm，宽50cm

Pottery Souvenir Badges

Gift of the King and Queen of Belgium, 1981

Length 80cm, width 50cm

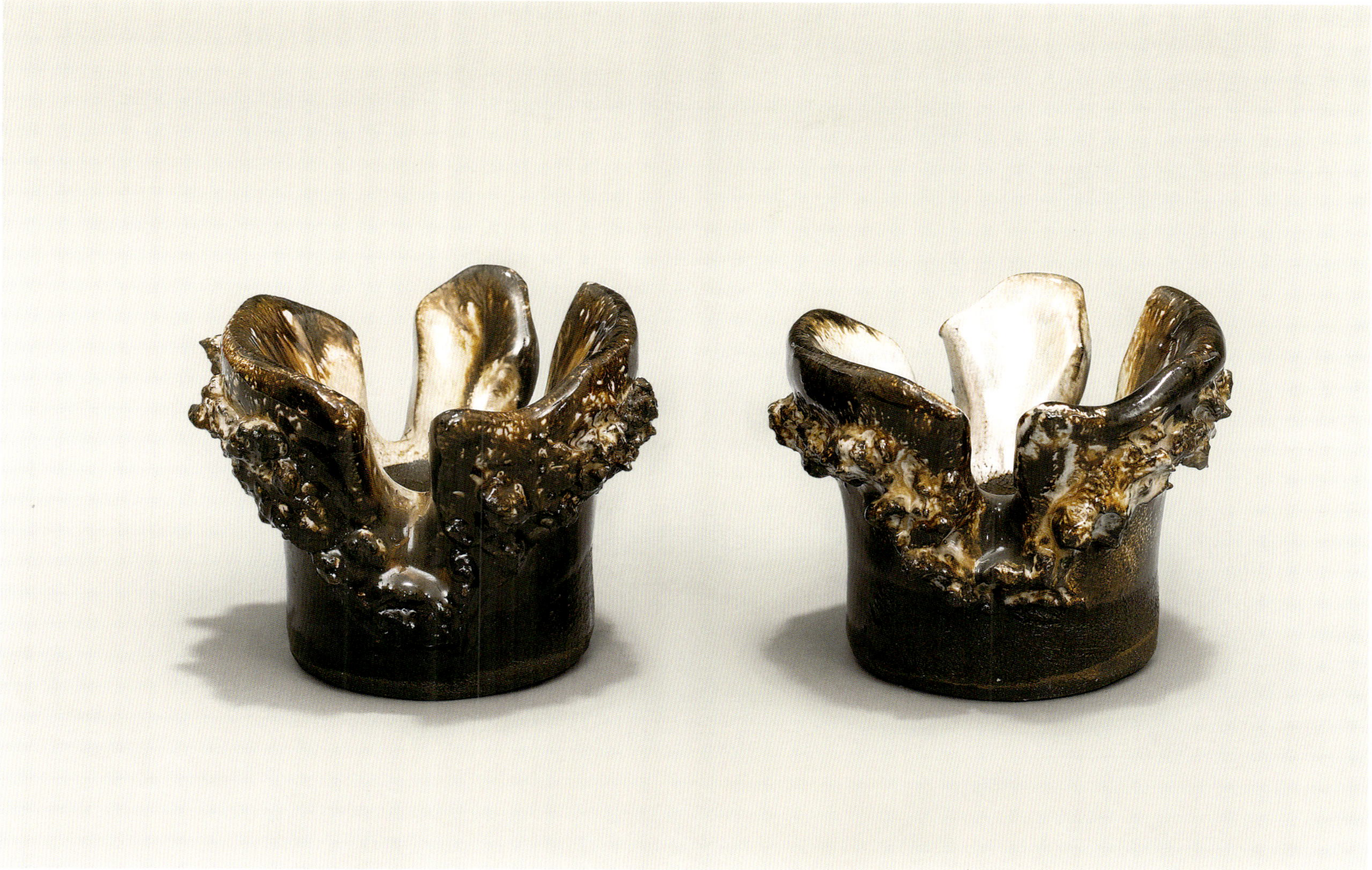

176

1982年冰岛文化教育部部长赠陶工艺烛台

高4.3 cm，口径5.2cm，底径3.8cm

Pottery Candlesticks

Gift of Minister of Culture and Education of Iceland, 1982

Height 4.3 cm, diameter of mouth 5.2cm, diameter of base 3.8cm

177

1990年苏联莫斯科文化基金代表团赠镀铜挂盘

高1.5cm，口径30cm，底径19 cm

Hanging Plate with Copper Plating

Gift of the Delegation of Culture Foundation of Moscow, the Soviet Union, 1990

Height 1.5cm, diameter of mouth 30cm, diameter of base 19cm

178

1983年荷兰鹿特丹市代表团赠“以战自强”市徽纪念牌

高22cm，长18.1cm，厚7cm

Memorial Plaque of Rotterdam's City Emblem "Sterker door strijd (striving to become stronger)"

Gift of the Delegation of Rotterdam, Netherlands, 1983

Height 22cm, length 18.1cm, thickness 7cm

鹿特丹市徽主要由狮子、盾牌、大坝和箴言组成，形成于16世纪。市徽下部代表13世纪中叶在鹿特河上建起的大坝。大坝上书写的箴言意为“以战自强”。1948年1月，威廉明娜女王将这句格言赐予鹿特丹，作为市政府徽章上的座右铭，以表彰鹿特丹人民在荷兰及全人类解放战争中所做出的贡献，象征鹿特丹人民从古至今与困难拼搏的勇气。

179

1979年卢森堡大公赠尼古拉斯·利耶（19世纪画家）烤画瓷盘

口径26.3cm

Porcelain Plate with Design of Nicolas Liez's Painting

Gift of the Grand Duke of Luxembourg, 1979

Diameter of mouth 26.3cm

瓷盘描绘的是卢森堡享有盛名的名胜古迹和奇特的城市风貌。卢森堡意为“小要塞城堡“，由130多座大小城堡组成。其中最大的卢森堡城，建于10世纪，曾是欧洲最强盛的城堡之一。

180

1982年卢森堡首相赠卢森堡国徽纪念牌

高7.9cm，宽5.1cm

Memorial Plaque of Luxembourg's National Emblem

Gift of the Premier of Luxembourg, 1982

Height 7.9cm, width 5.1cm

181（上）

1976年罗马尼亚军官休假组赠仿青铜烟碟（附座）

直径9.5cm

Bronze-imitating Ashtray (including base)

Gift of a Group of Romanian Military Officers on a Vacation, 1976

Diameter 9.5cm

182（下）

1977年罗马尼亚共产党工作者代表团赠人物雕塑挂屏

高15cm，宽20cm

Hanging Panel Decorated with High Relief Figures

Gift of the Delegation of the Communist Party Workers of Romania, 1977

Height 15cm, width 20cm

183

1978年罗马尼亚友人赠喀尔巴阡雄鹿链牌

直径7.6cm，链长72cm

Carpathian Stag Pendant with a Chain

Gift of Romanian Friends, 1978

Diameter 7.6cm, length of the chain 72cm

古代罗马尼亚达基亚人把鹿作为崇拜的神灵，以为世间之物多是这个“造物主”所恩赐的。罗马尼亚的许多民间风俗都与鹿相关，新娘陪嫁的东西也必须要有鹿才行，这样新婚夫妇的日子将会过得非常富有。关于鹿还有这样一种传说：14世纪末，瓦拉西亚的密尔西阿王子就是因为有鹿的帮助，才带领人民团结一致、同仇敌忾，与土耳其入侵者展开浴血奋战，终于赶走敌人取得了胜利。人们为了纪念这次具有意义的胜利，于是绘制鹿头的形象并铸在项链牌上，意为“光荣民族的标记”。所以以鹿头项链作为珍贵礼物送给对方，包含着一个简单而又深刻的哲理：生活的道路是坎坷的，只有克服重重障碍，日子才会过得美好。

184（上）

1978年挪威石油代表团赠北极熊玻璃雕塑

高9.3cm，宽6.5cm

Glass Sculpture of a Polar Bear

Gift of Petroleum Delegation of Norway, 1978

Height 9.3cm, width 6.5cm

185（下）

1985年挪威王储赠珐琅银碗

高3.4cm，口径13.9cm

Silver Bowl with Enamel

Gift of the Crown Prince of Norway, 1985

Height 3.4cm, diameter 13.9cm

186

1985年葡萄牙总统赠玻璃铃铛

通高17.5cm，底径9cm

Glass Bell

Gift of the President of Portugal, 1985

Overall height 17.5cm, diameter of base 9cm

187

1976年瑞典瑞中友联六月团赠斯德哥尔摩王宫瓷盘

口径21.6cm

Porcelain Plate Painted with Stockholm Palace

Gift of the June Touring Group of Sweden-China Friendship Association from Sweden, 1976

Diameter of mouth 21.6cm

188

1987年瑞士基亚索市市长赠街景写生

通高63cm，通宽51.3cm；画心高44.5cm，宽32.2cm

Landscape of Street

Gift of the Mayor of Chiasso, Switzerland, 1987

Overall height 63cm, overall width 51.3cm; painting: height 44.5cm, width 32.2cm

189

1987年瑞士基阿索市市长赠嵌一克千足金925银纪念牌

高8cm，宽12cm

92.5 Percent Silver Memorial Plate Inlaid with 1g Pure Gold

Gift of the Mayor of Chiasso, Switzerland, 1987

Height 8cm, width 12cm

190

1977年西德科隆德中友协会赠青花瓷酒壶

高12.5cm，口径5.5cm

Blue-and-white Porcelain Wine Jug

Gift of the Germany-China Friendship Association of Kolner, West Germany, 1977

Height 12.5cm, diameter of mouth 5.5cm

191

1976年意大利意中医学会赠罗马城徽雕塑

高7.6cm，通宽12cm，底座宽4.6cm

Female Wolf, the Emblem of Rome City

Gift of the Italy-China Medical Associatiom of Italy, 1976

Height 7.6cm, overall width 12cm, width of base 4.6cm

“母狼哺婴”塑像作为罗马城徽，代表了意大利高度璀璨的文化艺术，是意大利人馈赠的上等礼品。雕像中吸母狼乳汁的两个男婴相传是罗马城的缔造者罗姆洛和雷默斯。

这个雕塑取材于罗马城起源的传说：古时意大利有位国王叫依多米尔，他的弟弟阿木留斯篡夺王位，软禁国王，杀死王子，并强迫公主当女祭司。公主与战神相爱，生下一对孪生兄弟。阿木留斯为斩草除根，派人将孩子扔进台伯河。一只母狼赶来搭救，用乳汁哺育孩子。后来孩子被一对牧羊夫妇收养，取名为罗姆洛和雷默斯。他们长大后杀死阿木留斯，重新建都。罗姆洛争得王位后，以自己的名字命名新都为“罗马”。

192（上）

1984年意大利西西里政府赠三曲腿美杜莎金属雕像

高14cm，宽14cm

Metal Statue of Triskelion Medusa

Gift of Sicilian Autonomous Region Government, Italy, 1984

Height 14cm, width 14cm

193（下）

1991年意大利总理安德雷奥蒂赠基吉宫（现意大利总理府）铜版画银盒

高3cm，长18.2cm，宽11cm

Silver Box with Copperplate Etching of Palazzo Chigi (the premier's office nowadays)

Gift of Giulio Andreotti, the Premier of Italy, 1991

Height 3cm, length 18.2cm, width 11cm

出版统筹　姜革文　张　明
责任编辑　贾宁宁
美术编辑　姚明聚　王玲芳
责任技编　王增元

英文翻译　李宏霞　贾宁宁
作品拍摄　陈诗文

图书在版编目（CIP）数据

外邦粹礼：桂林博物馆藏外宾礼品：汉、英 / 唐春松主编．—桂林：广西师范大学出版社，2015.1
ISBN 978-7-5495-6079-0

Ⅰ．①外…　Ⅱ．①唐…　Ⅲ．①外交－礼品－桂林市－图集　Ⅳ．①D827.673-64

中国版本图书馆 CIP 数据核字（2014）第 276553 号

广西师范大学出版社出版发行
（广西桂林市中华路 22 号　邮政编码：541001
网址：http://www.bbtpress.com）
出版人：何林夏
全国新华书店经销
北京雅昌艺术印刷有限公司印刷
（北京市顺义区天竺空港工业区 A 区天纬四街 7 号　邮编：101312）
开本：787 mm × 1 092 mm　1/8
印张：22.5　　　字数：270 千字
2015 年 1 月第 1 版　　　2015 年 1 月第 1 次印刷
定价：360. 00 元